STOCKWELL-MUDD LIBRARIES

D1483191

THE JUDGMENT
OF THE NATIONS

THE
JUDGMENT OF
THE NATIONS

by

CHRISTOPHER DAWSON

1942

SHEED & WARD

NEW YORK

COPYRIGHT, 1942, BY SHEED & WARD, INC.

First Printing, September, 1942
Second Printing, January, 1943

BR
115
.P7D35

66135

MANUFACTURED IN THE UNITED STATES OF AMERICA
BY THE HADDON CRAFTSMEN, INC., SCRANTON, PA.

CONTENTS

Part I

THE DISINTEGRATION OF
WESTERN CIVILIZATION

The Hour of Darkness

A HUNDRED years is a relatively short period. It does not even exceed the span of a single human life. Yet the last hundred years have changed human life more completely than any period in the history of the world. It is as though the stream of time had been transformed from a slow flowing river to a roaring cataract. A hundred years ago the greater part of the human race was still living as it had always lived. The Far East was still a closed world as remote in thought from Europe as though it had been a different planet while the Far West was still empty, and tropical Africa still unknown. In the space of three generations the whole world has been opened up, brought together and changed. There has been a breathless advance in population, wealth and knowledge. The cities have not only increased in numbers and size: they have drawn the world together into a single society. The time is approaching when the cities become one city—a Babylon which sets its mark on the mind of every man and woman and imposes the same pattern of behaviour on every human activity.

In a sense this development has fulfilled and even exceeded the hopes of the men of a century ago. It was the heyday of liberal optimism when the romantic despair of the previous generation had given way to a faith in the boundless possibilities of science, material progress and political freedom.

> . . . in the march of mind,
> In the steamship, in the railway, in the thoughts
> that shake mankind.

Yet even the most optimistic failed to realize the speed and scale of the movement that was beginning to gather momentum and which was to lead in so short a time to the conquest of time and space and the complete subjugation of nature to human purpose. For a generation from 1840 to 1870 things went very much as the Liberals had expected, disappointing the visionary hopes of idealists like Mazzini and fully satisfying the progressive nineteenth century public opinion which found its embodiment in statesmen like Cavour and Gladstone. Then for forty years there was a period of uneasy peace, in which men gradually lost their faith in the ideals of nineteenth century liberalism, though material prosperity and scientific knowledge continued to increase. In that restless calm when the energies of the western world seemed absorbed in money-making and the exploitation of the weaker peoples, a few prophetic voices were heard announcing the approaching end of the age—but they were the voices of men possessed, like Nietzsche and Dostoevski, who had no place in that fool's paradise which is called the real world.

But during the last thirty years this artificial reality has collapsed like a house of cards; the demons which haunted the brains of those outcasts have invaded the world of men and become its masters. The old landmarks of good and evil and truth and falsehood have been swept away and civilization is driving before the storm of destruction like a dismasted and helmless ship. The evils which the nineteenth century thought that it had banished for ever—proscription and persecution, torture and slavery and the fear of sudden death—have returned and with them new terrors which the past did not know. We have discovered that evil too is a progressive force and that the modern world provides unlimited prospects for its development.

Thus it is no accident that the period that has seen the culmination of the modern development of scientific and economic power should have brought Western civilization to the brink of ruin. For it is our power that is our destruction, and the world is drunk and poisoned with power, as primitive peoples have been poisoned by the gin and germs and gunpowder of a more advanced civilization.

There is in fact an even wider gulf between the external conditions of our life and those of our ancestors a century ago than there was between the civilization of the Spanish Conquistadors and that of the natives of the New World. The motor car and the aeroplane represent a far more revolutionary change in the relation of man to his environment than the coming of the armoured horseman who destroyed the civilization of Mexico and Peru. But the change has been too sudden for men to adapt themselves to the new conditions. Human nature changes slowly and the men who have conquered time and

space and acquired almost unlimited material power
are no more super-men than were their great-grand-
fathers of 1840. Yet they have been made super-men
in spite of themselves—they have been taken from
the plough and the cobbler's bench and have been
given power which even the deified autocrats of the
old world empires never possessed.

These are the conditions that have led to the rise
of the totalitarian state. It is an attempt to solve the
problem of mass power by force and thus it produces
a new series of tensions and conflict which intensify
the destructive character of the crisis. The problems
of power cannot be solved by power alone, nor can
they be solved by science, since science has become
the servant of power. Liberty and reason are being
destroyed by the powers that they created and humanity is slipping blindly and helplessly towards the
abyss. For humanity cannot save itself by its own
efforts. When it is left to itself it perishes, and the
greater its power and material resources, the more
complete is the catastrophe.

This is the truth which was recognized by every
civilization that the world has known but which has
been forgotten or denied by modern man in the in-
toxication of his newly acquired power. Nevertheless
it has not been left without a witness. Throughout
the last hundred years the Church has not ceased to
maintain the principle of the dependence of human
society and human law on an order which transcends
politics and economics, and to warn men of the inevitable catastrophe that must result from the attempt
to create a civilization which knew no law but man's

own needs and ambitions. In the first of the three periods of which I have spoken these warnings were summarily dismissed as mere reactionary obscurantism. Nevertheless, when Piux IX condemned Liberalism, he did so, not because it freed the nations from despotism and limited the powers of the state, but because he saw in it the denial of the subordination of human society to divine law and the assertion of a new principle of unrestricted power which was more far-reaching than any royal prerogative.*

The implications of this principle became still clearer in the second period, when the liberal idealism of Mazzini and Lamartine gave place to the triumphant secularism of the later nineteenth century state. It was then that Leo XIII summed up Catholic social principles in that great series of encyclicals which are the classical expression of the ideals of Christian humanism and Christian liberalism that have been the inspiration of Western culture. But his warnings were equally disregarded. When in 1878 the Pope declared that the human race was being hurried onwards to the verge of ruin and warned society to prepare for the impending crisis before it was too late, his words made no impression on a civilization that was growing in material prosperity and still relatively stable. It is only during the last thirty years that the world has awaked to the reality of the dangers of which the Papacy has spoken so long. During the last three pontificates the true issues have been revealed with appalling

* Cf. Leo XIII on false liberalism in The Pope and the People, p. 88.

clarity, and the Church no longer seems a disregarded
witness of forgotten truth, but stands at the very
heart of the struggle in which every human being is
involved. Today the enemy is not the humanitarian
liberalism which was a kind of secularized version
of Christian moral idealism. It is a new power which
tramples every human right and ideal under foot.
Under the shadow of this threat the partial conflicts
that have divided Western culture no longer have the
same meaning, and the cause of God and the cause of
humanity have become one. The law of charity is not
alien to human nature and does not stand in opposition to the ideals of freedom and social progress
that have inspired Western culture in modern times.
On the contrary, it is the only law that can save
mankind from the iron law of power which destroys
the weak by violence and the strong by treachery.
For the new paganism has nothing in common with
the poetical idealization of Hellenic myth by the humanists and classicists of recent centuries: it is the
unloosing of the powers of the abyss—the dark forces
that have been chained by a thousand years of Chris-
tion civilization and which have now been set free
to conquer the world. For the will to power is also
the will to destruction, and in the last event it becomes the will to self-destruction.

In these dark times there must be many who feel
tempted to despair when they see the ruin of the
hopes of peace and progress that inspired the Liberal
idealism of the last century, and the perversion of the
great achievements of human knowledge and power
to serve the devilish forces of destruction. Never,

perhaps, has a civilization suffered such a total subversion of its own standards and values while its material power and wealth remained almost intact, and in many respects greater than ever.

To Christians, however, the shock and the disillusionment should be less severe than to those who have put their faith in the nineteenth-century gospel of secular progress. For the Christian faith never minimized the reality of the forces of evil in history and society, as well as in the life of the individual, and it has prepared men's minds to face the extreme consequences of the external triumph of evil, and the apparent defeat of good. Yet none the less it is no defeatist philosophy; it is a triumphant affirmation of life—of eternal life victorious over death, of the kingdom of God prevailing over the rulers of this world of darkness.

Fifteen centuries ago the ancient world was faced with a crisis that threatened civilization with destruction almost at the moment when the Church had won the victory over paganism. For one thousand years the Mediterranean world had lived securely in the light of Hellenic culture. Now its sun had set, and the darkness and cold of the barbarous north descended on the world. The East German warrior peoples driven from South Russia and the Danube, by the advance of the Mongol hordes from beyond the Volga, broke through the defense of the Empire and wrecked the imposing fabric of Roman order. Yet St. Augustine had his answer. He could stand above the conflict because though he was a loyal Roman and a scholar who realized the value of Greek

thought, he regarded these things as temporary and
accidental. He lived not by the light of Athens and
Alexandria, but by a new light, that had suddenly
dawned on the world from the East only a few centuries earlier. Imperial Rome was, after all, the
daughter of Babylon, the incarnation of human pride
and material wealth, the persecutor of the saints, and
the oppressor of the poor. Man's true destinies were
realized elsewhere, in Jerusalem, the City of God,
which was being built up through all the ruin and
destruction of human kingdoms and empires by the
irresistible momentum of a divine purpose.

But for us, today, the answer is far more difficult.
For the civilization which has been undermined,
and is now threatened by total subversion, is a Christian civilization, built on the spiritual values and
religious ideals of St. Augustine and his like; and its
adversary is not the simple barbarism of alien peoples
who stand on a lower cultural level, but new Powers
armed with all the resources of modern scientific
technique, which are inspired by a ruthless will to
power, that recognizes no law save that of their own
strength. This is almost a reversal of the situation
envisaged by St. Augustine. In his day the world was
falling, and the gates of the Church stood open as a
city of refuge for a defeated humanity. Today the
world is strong: and it has no pity for weakness and
suffering. It has no use for Christianity which it
despises as the most dangerous form of escapism and
defeatism. It has its own religion—a religion which
reverses the Christian moral values, which says
"Blessed are the strong for they shall possess the

earth," but which, no less than Christianity, demands unlimited sacrifices and an undivided allegiance of the whole man. Thus the situation that Christians have to face today has more in common with that described by the author of the Apocalypse, than with the age of St. Augustine. The world is strong, and it has evil masters. But these masters are not vicious autocrats like Nero or Domitian. They are the engineers of the mechanism of world power: a mechanism that is more formidable than anything the ancient world knew, because it is not confined to external means, like the despotisms of the past, but uses all the resources of modern psychology to make the human soul the motor of its dynamic purpose.

Hence, while the fundamental Augustinian principles of the Two Loves and the Two Cities retain their validity, they have assumed a new form in these times, unlike anything in the previous experience of the Church. For today a deliberate attempt is being made to unify and energize human society from its lower depths: to bring Jerusalem—the spirit of Man as the vessel of the Spirit of God—into servitude to Babylon—the spirit of man degraded into the blind instrument of a demonic will to power. There is no room here to discuss the origin and development of this evil. It is sufficient to say that the revolutionary tendencies in modern civilization which were originally inspired by a positive humanitarian optimism have become perverted into a "Revolution of Destruction." And the main cause of this, as Nietzsche pointed out, has been the loss of the Christian moral values which "prevented man from despising himself as man, from turning against life, and from being driven to despair by knowledge."

For when once morality has been deprived of its religious and metaphysical foundations, it inevitably becomes subordinated to lower ends; and when these ends are negative, as in revolution and war, the whole scale of moral values becomes reversed. It is possible to understand how this moral nihilism may be combined with a kind of fanatical idealism in a subterranean revolutionary movement. But it becomes a much more evil thing when it is adopted as the creed of a Government, and is used by the ruling power to defend violence and injustice, when the revolutionary terrorism of the secret society blends with the repressive terrorism of the secret police to produce a new totalitarian technique of government by force and by fear which undermines the psychological foundations of moral freedom.

From the Christian point of view, the most serious feature of the situation is that evil has become, as it were, de-personalized, separated from individual passion and appetite, and exalted above humanity into a sphere in which all moral values are confused and transformed. The great terrorists from Robespierre and St. Just to Dzershinski have not been immoral men, but rigid puritans who did evil coldly, by principle, without any thought of personal advantage, while the new mass dictatorships associate the highest and lowest qualities of human nature—self-sacrifice and boundless devotion, as well as unlimited violence and vindictiveness—in the assertion of their will to power.

This is the new evil that has spread from Russia, westward, into the very heart of Europe. It is no longer necessarily associated with Communism. On the contrary, it spreads by opposition, even more than by imitation. As soon as men decide that all means are permitted to fight an evil, then their good becomes indistinguishable from the evil that they set out to destroy. The subordination of morals to politics, the reign of terror and the technique of propaganda and psychological aggression can be used by any Power or Party that is bold enough to abandon moral scruples and plunge into the abyss.

This is the greatest difficulty that faces us at the present time. For it is an evil that thrives by war, and the necessity of opposing the spirit of unlimited aggression by force of arms, creates the atmosphere which is most favourable to its growth. Hence we have the hard task of carrying on simultaneously a war on two fronts. We have to oppose, by arms, the aggression of the external enemy, and at the same time to resist the enemy within—the growth in our own society of the evil power that we are fighting against. And this second war is the more dangerous of the two, since it may be lost by victory as well as by defeat, and the very fact that we are driven to identify the evil with that manifestation of it that threatens our national existence, tends to blind us to the more insidious tendencies in the same direction that are to be found in our own social order. The disintegration of Western culture under the moral and economic strain of war is not a danger that can be lightly dismissed. Nor can it be accepted by Christians in the same spirit in which they accepted the fall of the Roman Empire. For that was an external disaster, which left the sources of spiritual vitality unimpaired, while this is a spiritual catastrophe which strikes directly at the moral foundations of our society, and destroys not the outward form of civilization but the soul of man which is the beginning and end of all human culture.

2

Democracy and Total War

WHEN the war began there was a tendency in many neutral quarters to minimize the importance of the issues, to view it as a war in the old style between certain European powers in which only their own national interests and prestige were at stake, or even to regard it as a sham fight put up to cover a strategic retreat to new diplomatic positions.

Today it is no longer possible for anyone to deceive himself with such illusions. This "phoney war" has revealed itself as a total war which takes no account of national sovereignty or international conventions or human rights, and the conflagration spreads with such rapidity that no state is so strong or so remote that it can reckon on remaining isolated. Whatever the issue may be, it must affect the whole world and the future of every people and civilization.

Much has been written on the war aims and the peace aims of the Allies, but the real issue is a very simple one: to check the power of the greatest military machine in the world before it conquers Europe and dominates the world.

Thus whatever their faults and whatever the defects of their own social systems, Britain and America stand today as the bulwark of the freedom of the world. If that bulwark is broken, no one knows what will come next—universal chaos or universal slavery. In any case it is foolishness to suppose that the consequences can be limited to Europe. The Atlantic world itself is a unity, on which the Pacific world in turn depends. If the two pillars of Atlantis are broken, the whole of the Western hemisphere will be shaken.

Nor can the effects of such a catastrophe be limited to politics and economics. They involve profound changes in the character of civilization such as have only occurred in the past in the case of a religious revolution. For the most characteristic feature of the totalitarian system against which we are fighting is its claim to control men's minds as well as their bodies, and in order to enforce this claim it mobilizes all the resources of the new black arts of mass suggestion and propaganda. It wages war not only by military and economic means, but by spiritual weapons that are directed against the mind and will of the peoples who oppose it—and not of them alone, but of all peoples whose sympathies may affect the issue of the struggle—that is to say every people in the world.

This immense extension of the character of the war not only makes nonsense of the old conception of neutrality together with all the other established laws and conventions that guarded international relations, but involves moral issues to which no Christian can be indifferent. In the past it was possible to regard war as an external misfortune, like plague and famine, which must be endured as a divine judgement, but which did not affect man's personal responsibility or his religious freedom. On the contrary, the evils of war often strengthened the appeal of religion by turning men's minds from earthly strife to the vision of eternal peace. But total war respects none of these things and leaves no spiritual value intact. It treats religion itself as another weapon in its armory, and if we take refuge in pacifism, we find that pacifism is being exploited in the same way as a useful tool for weakening resistance and disintegrating national morale.

The massive drive for power which constitutes totalitarianism is abolishing the limits which had been imposed by centuries of Christianity and civilization on the primitive instincts of violence and aggressiveness. But these limits are not only necessary to the preservation of individual freedom, they are no less essential to social order; and when they are destroyed, there is nothing left between the naked human soul and the forces of destruction. Thus the present war with its unlimited destructiveness and its utter disregard of legal and moral restrictions is only the external symptom of the disease from which not only Germany and not only Europe but the whole world is suffering.

What is the source of this evil? It has certainly not been invented by Herr Hitler and his colleagues. They are its creatures, not its creators. They are only men who have been carried to power on the crest of the wave of destruction, like the leaders of the Convention during the French Revolution, the lawyers and journalists who appeared out of nowhere and changed the face of Europe and disappeared as suddenly as they had arisen. But whereas the driving force of the French Revolution was an immense wave of idealism and hope in the future, the new revolution is a movement of disintegration and despair which derives its strength from the liquidation of the ideals on which the nineteenth-century world had set its hopes.

The view that modern civilization was inevitably tending towards such a catastrophe is by no means new. Already in the nineteenth century it was the central theme of Nietzsche's philosophy of culture which has had so deep an influence on both German and Russian thought. Nor does Nietzsche stand alone. An older contemporary of his in Russia, Constantine Leontiev, who is the subject of M. Berdyaev's latest work, passed a very similar judgment on Western culture.

"That far too mobile order," he writes, "which gave mankind the nineteenth century ideas of progress, equality, and emancipation is most unstable, and . . . must end either in a universal catastrophe or in a slow and profound transformation of human societies on the basis of completely new principles— principles not only no longer liberal, but, on the contrary, extremely repressive and tyrannical. Perhaps slavery will return once more, assuming a different form, very likely that of a rigid subservience of persons to large and small communities and of them in their turn, to the State." "In any case this new culture will be very oppressive for many, and the men of the twentieth century, which is already so near to us, far from kneading it from the sugar and rose-

water of measured freedom and humanity will compound it of something else, of something unfamiliar
or even terrifying," so that "the life of these *new
men* must ultimately prove to be far more oppressive
and unhealthy than the life of good conscientious
monks in austere monasteries."*

This remarkable forecast or rather prophecy has
been fulfilled almost to the letter. During the last
twenty years liberal democracy has met with one defeat after another. Over a great part of the world
we have seen the complete abrogation of those liberties which the nineteenth century regarded as the
basis of modern civilization and the establishment
of a new social order which denies the most elementary human rights and destroys whole classes and
peoples as ruthlessly as any Oriental despotism in the
past. And this has come about not by the triumph
of the "reactionary" or conservative forces in Western
society, but by their defeat and the triumph of their
enemies. It has been the work of mass movements
and revolutionary parties led by men of the people.

It is true that this movement began when liberal
democracy was weakest and has won its chief triumphs
in countries which had been accustomed for centuries
to the rigid discipline of a theocratic autocracy or a
military monarchy. In Russia, above all, Western
democracy was a foreign importation and not only
reactionaries, like Leontiev, but socialists like Herzen
and anarchists like Bakunin, hated the top hat and
frock-coat of the Western bourgeois as the drab livery
of servitude to alien ideals which were more foreign

---

* Nicholas Berdyaev. *Leontiev* (Geoffrey Bles 1940) pp. 100-102.

to their traditions and instincts than even the serfdom and obscurantism of Czarism.

It is therefore important to distinguish two elements in the modern reaction against liberal democracy. There is the reaction that has arisen out of democracy itself, as a result of the progress of man's organization and the mechanization of our culture which has destroyed the economic and social basis of liberal individualism; and, secondly, there is the national reaction of those countries which had no native democratic tradition and which had accepted liberal ideas as part of the material culture of Western Europe, which they felt to be the symbol not only of progress, but also of foreign exploitation.

It was only when these two elements coalesced in the defeat and revolution of the post-war period that they gave birth to the new totalitarian order which is now threatening the existence of democracy in Western Europe and in the world. As in the nineteenth century Western democracy asserted its hegemony by a process of economic and ideological penetration, by Free Trade and the free press and by the propagation of liberal ideas, so today the new totalitarian régime is seeking to extend its domination by its own methods—by the organization and disciplining of the masses and by the beating down of all opposition within and without by a combination of psychological pressure and military aggression.

Is Western democracy strong enough to resist this attack, or is Western Europe destined to follow the path taken by Germany and Russia and to undergo a totalitarian revolution? The answer does not de-

pend on military factors alone, for even success in
war would not of itself prevent the decline of democracy if modern conditions are unfavourable to
its survival, while on the other hand, if the foundations of Western democracy are sound, even a military defeat would not destroy it.

It is necessary, in the first place, to understand
what we mean by democracy, and secondly, to distinguish between what is living and what is dead in
the democratic tradition that we have inherited from
the nineteenth century. By democracy we mean not
merely self-government or popular government, but
rather that particular form of self-government which
was based on the ideal of personal liberty and which
was embodied in representative or parliamentary
institutions. This particular form of democracy is
peculiar to modern Western civilization and is spe-
cially associated with the three great political nations
of the West, England, France and the United States,
from whom it spread in the course of the nineteenth
century over almost the whole of the civilized world.
But though it only attained its full development as
a result of the three Western revolutions—the English Revolutions of 1642-1688, the American Revolution, and the French Revolution—its roots lie deep
in the soil of Western Christendom so that it is impossible to understand it aright apart from its religious and cultural background. Thus the Western
ideal of liberty which is the inspiration of the whole
democratic tradition is not a mere consequence of the
new political institutions. As Burke wrote, it permeated the whole Christian order of Christian society

and "arose not from the laws of the state (in which it flourished more from neglect than attention), but from the system of manners and the habitudes of life." Above all it derived its strength from the Christian belief in the absolute and unique value of the human soul which infinitely transcends all the wealth and the power and the glory of the world.

The political and social consequences of such a belief are twofold. On the one hand it produces the ascetic or other-worldly attitude—the depreciation of earthly goods and worldly power, and the transference of the center of thought and action to the supertemporal and religious sphere. But on the other hand it also tended to assert itself within the social and political order by the modification of social types and institutions in a Christian sense.

Thus, just as Christian monarchy became a very different thing from the barbarian kingships from which it was historically descended, so Christian freedom combined and transformed the elements of barbaric freedom and classical citizenship into something new. The deepest spiritual root of Western democracy is to be found neither in the blood brotherhood of warrior tribesmen nor in the civic privileges of the city state, but in the spiritual reversal of values which caused men to honour poverty and suffering and to see in the poor man the image of Christ Himself.

This sense of Christian liberty and Christian democracy (to use Leo XIII's expression) was diffused throughout the whole body of Christendom and formed the spiritual background of a social order

which from an external point of view often appears
extremely hierarchic and authoritarian. In Eastern
Europe, owing largely to the Oriental imperialisms
to which it was so long subjected, this background
was so far removed from political realities that the
Christian social consciousness expressed itself in mys-
tical or apocalyptic terms. In the West, however, the
social order was more plastic and more organically
related to the beliefs and ideals of the people. In
fact, no civilization, not even that of ancient Greece,
has ever undergone such a continuous and profound
process of change as Western Europe has done during
the last nine hundred years. It is impossible to explain this fact in purely economic terms by a materialistic interpretation of history. The principle of
change has been a spiritual one and the progress
of Western civilization is intimately related to the
dynamic ethos of Western Christianity, which has
gradually made Western man conscious of his moral
responsibility and his duty to change the world. This
claim is implicit in the Christian view of the world:
indeed it was already stated in the most explicit terms
by St. Paul: "Do you not know that the Saints shall
judge the world? And if the world shall be judged by
you, are you unworthy to judge the smallest matters?
Know you not that we shall judge Angels, how much
more secular things?"* The history of Christendom
is the story of the progressive vindication of this
tremendous claim which not only made the Church a
far more dynamic social force than any other religious body that the world has known, but diffused its

* I Corinthians VI, 2-3.

influence through the whole of Western civilization and affected spheres of thought and action far removed from the direct influence of religion.

It was not, in fact, until after the end of the Middle Ages when the unity of medieval Christendom had been lost that the full effects of this revolutionary spiritual change were felt. Thus the rise of Western democracy like that of Western humanism was not really the creation of a new secular culture but were the results of centuries which had ploughed the virgin soil of the West and scattered the new seed broadcast over the face of the earth. No doubt the seed was often mixed with cockle, or choked with briars, or sown on barren soil where it withered, nevertheless the harvest was good and the world still lives upon it.

We must therefore realize that when we say we are fighting for democracy, we are not fighting merely for certain political institutions or even political principles. Still less are we fighting for the squalid prosperity of modern industrialism which was the outcome of the economic liberalism of the last century. What we have to defend is, to quote Cardinal Liénart's words, "a human and Christian civilization, built with infinite patience": a work to which many different races and peoples and schools of thought have contributed century after century.

And in spite of the conflict that has marked its development it has been a work of unity; for Christianity and humanism and social freedom are not conflicting ideas that have alternately dominated the European mind, they have a spiritual affinity that was not apparent to the reformers and revolutionaries who were enveloped in the dust of conflict, but which is now becoming visible when all of them are threatened alike by inhuman forces that have no kinship with any of them.

The great danger we have to face is due to the absence of a clear understanding of this spiritual community. European culture has passed through a period of individualism and atomization which has prepared the way for the more formidable disintegration of nihilism which threatens us today. Hence it is all too easy in the shipwreck of Europe for each separate party or group to attempt to shift the blame for the disaster onto the shoulders of the rest or even to exploit it in their own interests, somewhat as in the breakup of the Roman Empire every provincial army struck out for their own hand and used the common danger as an opportunity for their own aggrandizement. The enemies of Europe are quite conscious of this weakness and they are ready to exploit the divisions and dissensions between parties and sects and classes and schools of thought in order to produce an atmosphere of universal distrust and disintegration which will prepare the way for their work of destruction.

This is the cause of the gravity of the present situation. Western democracy is not only fighting a battle on two fronts with the rival totalitarianisms of the Right and the Left. It is at the same time being undermined from within by a process of disintegration which saps our vitality and weakens our power of resistance.

It is inevitable that we should seek to meet these dangers by an immense concentration of effort which unites all the forces of the nation—military, economic and psychological—in the common cause. Does this mean that it is impossible for democracy to defeat totalitarianism without becoming totalitarian itself? The great problem that the democratic states have to solve is how to reconcile the needs of mass organization and mechanized power, which finds its extreme expression in total war, with the principles of freedom and justice and humanity from which their spiritual strength is derived. There seems to be an inherent contradiction between the totalitarian technique which is a modernized form of the old tradition of absolute government, based on military discipline, the repression of thought and the régime of secret police, and the democratic system which involves the limitation of the power of the executive, government by discussion and voluntary co-operation, and the freedom of public opinion; and no amount of scientific planning can overcome this opposition. Nevertheless it has yet to be proved that a system, which is of its nature more adaptable than the rigid order of absolutism, is incapable of meeting the challenge of the totalitarian state and the new conditions of warfare.

It is true that war, which is a state of organized violence, is by its very nature opposed to the ideal of personal liberty under the Rule of Law and the system of government by discussion which are characteristic of Western democracy. But war, viewed in this absolute sense, is no less opposed to Christianity and indeed to any high form of civilized life. War, in fact, is barbarism and "the nations that delight in war"—"gentes quae in sua feritate confidunt"—were regarded by Christian antiquity as "barbarians" in the strict sense and representatives of the opposite social principle to that which was embodied in the order of Christendom.

Again and again the existence of Christendom was threatened by the assaults of this external barbarism which often infected Christian society itself with the spirit of brutal violence and the lust of conquest. Nevertheless Christendom survived the dark ages in which the only law was that of the sword, and the nations who accepted the gospel of peace and worshipped the Cross of Christ proved stronger than the worshippers of the war god.

And so it may be in the conflict between the new barbarism, which sacrifices every human value to the conquest of power, and Western democracy, which is the heir of Christendom. Democracy will not be destroyed either by military defeat or by the discipline and organization which it has to impose on itself in order to gain the victory, if it can maintain its spiritual value and preserve itself from the dangers of demoralization and disintegration. But this is not an easy task. For upwards of two hundred years the mind of Western culture has been divided against itself by the conflict between religion and rationalism, as it had been divided in the preceding centuries between Catholicism and Protestantism. But this conflict which divided the modern world was not really one between the religious and the anti-religious forces

in our civilization, but a conflict between two rival
religions: traditional Christianity on the one hand,
and, on the other, a secular religion of human progress which aroused no less enthusiastic faith and
boundless hope and love of humanity than any religious revival. All the "progressive" movements—
the Enlightenment, Liberalism, Democracy, Humani-
tarianism, Socialism—aligned themselves on the side
of the new religion, while the "reactionaries," the
defenders of the old order—royalists, traditionalists,
conservatives—rallied to the defense of traditional
Christianity and to the Church as an institution.

This alignment of forces was most sharply defined
among Catholic peoples, above all in Southern Europe. Among Protestants and especially in England
the division was less clear cut, for there were all kinds
of gradations of religious opinion from the Tory
High Churchman to the Unitarian. Indeed the driving power behind English political Liberalism was
the Nonconformist conscience which from a purely
religious point of view was rigidly conservative and
traditionalist. Nevertheless, even in England, and in
the United States, the intellectual leaders of the religion of progress, such as Bentham and the two
Mills, Robert Owen and Herbert Spencer, Thomas
Huxley and John Morley, were hostile to traditional
Christianity and in more or less close contact with
the Liberals and Socialists of the Continent.

But during the last thirty years this alignment of
forces has ceased to represent the realities of the
situation. A new power has arisen which is no less
hostile to the liberal and humanitarian ideals of the

apostles of progress than to the historic faith of Christendom. The world has been slow to grasp the nature of this power, for it has little in common with the religious and political theories that have governed mankind in the past. Its strength is derived not from ideas or beliefs, but from the negation of them, from the blind forces of destruction that lie deep in the human soul and which have now erupted from below the surface of civilization like a sleeping volcano that bursts into destructive activity:

Wie ein vulkanischer Berg lag er im weiten. Manchmal
Flammend. Manchmal im Rauch. Traurig und göttlich.
Und nun aufstand er: steht: höher
Als stehende Türme, höher
Als die geatmete Luft unseres sonstigen Tags.
Steht. Übersteht. Und wir? Glühen in Eines zusammen
In ein neues Geschöpf, das er tödlich belebt.*

It is particularly difficult for the Englishman to comprehend the importance of this "revolution of destruction" (to use Herr Rauschning's phrase), for nihilism is a phenomenon that is very remote from our national temperament and traditions, so that we are apt to dismiss the direct vision of it that was given to Dostoevski or to Nietzsche as a metaphysical nightmare. Nevertheless the fact remains that the revolt against moral idealism and humanist culture and Liberal democracy is no less of an historical reality than the Reformation or the French Revolution, and as those movements affected the whole of Western culture though they were originally associated with a

* R. M. Rilke, *Fünf Gesänge* (August 1914).

Albion
College
Library

particular country, so is it with the new "anti-religion." As Dr. Borkenau has shown so clearly in his recent book,* National Socialism in Germany, like Bolshevism in Russia, is a specific national reaction to a worldwide state of mind. In Germany it has taken a distinctively military and aggressive turn, owing to the peculiar violence and rapidity of the dissolution of the nineteenth-century order that followed the collapse of the Empire in 1918, and to the fact that the nineteenth-century order as we know it in the West with its parliamentary Liberalism and its economic individualism was a superficial development in comparison with the military tradition which had built up the Prussian state by war and for war to a degree that no other European state has been. It has therefore proved easier in Germany to yoke the whole force of the state to the revolutionary will to power and to launch it like an avalanche on the plane of external aggression. In the same way the pagan character of the Nazi ethic is not without its historical background. For while Western Germany formed part of the body of Christendom from the beginning, the conversion of Eastern Germany and especially the Baltic provinces was not only late in time, but was carried out by war and violence, so that the disunity and lack of balance that marks the German national temperament is rooted in the racial and historical origins of the German national being. The spirit of the old gods was imperfectly exorcised by the sword and it has continued to haunt the background of the German mind.

* *The Totalitarian Enemy,* by Franz Borkenau. Faber & Faber.

In the West, on the other hand, paganism died a natural death and has left no trace behind it. When we speak of the followers of the new religion of progress as "pagans" we are using the word in a different sense. Locke and Franklin, Rousseau and Lamartine, J. S. Mill and Guizot and de Tocqueville were a great deal further removed from paganism than were their medieval ancestors. They were indeed still Christians of a sort, even though they no longer believed that they believed. Today this type of sublimated Christianity is discredited. In fact it has been the object of sharper and more intense criticism than dogmatic Christianity. It is easy to understand that this change has been welcomed by pious Christians as a sign of religious revival and of a reawakening of religious faith. It is, however, nothing of the kind. It simply means that the disintegrating movement which was first directed against institutional and dogmatic Christianity has now been concentrated against the Christian ethos and the moral and humanitarian idealism that was derived from it. This is not surprising since in Western Europe institutional Christianity has long ceased to dominate society and culture, whereas the sublimated Christianity of the Liberals and the humanitarians in spite of its vague and unorganized character was the working religion of Western democracy and exercised a real influence over the social consciousness. Nevertheless Christians have no reason to look on the defeat of this spirit with complacency or indifference. The cause of God and the cause of man are one. Christians were justified in condemning the separation of the ideals of justice and liberty and reason from their foundations in Christian faith and practice. But these ideals are not empty abstractions. They are the foundations of human life; and when they are undermined, the whole edifice of civilization is dissolved in disintegration and chaos.

The Religious Origins of European Disunity

THE fundamental issue that lies behind the present war and has to a great extent produced it is that of the disintegration of Western culture. Not that civilization is faced by the prospect of a new dark age in the same way that the Roman world was at the time of the barbarian invasions, it is rather a disintegration from within such as Rome experienced centuries before the coming of the barbarians when her material power was at its height. We are in a position to understand the state of mind of Tacitus when he wrote the preface to his histories.

We are entering [he says] upon the history of a period rich in disasters, gloomy with wars, rent with seditions and savage in its very hours of peace—there was defilement of sacred rites, adulteries in high places, the sea was crowded with exiles, island rocks drenched with murder . . . all was one delirium of hate and terror; slaves were bribed to betray their masters, freedmen their patrons. He who had no enemy was destroyed by his friend.

The explanation of that process of disintegration was relatively simple. It was due to the impossibility of adapting the liberties that had been developed in the limited field of the city state to the conditions of a world empire. Our own problems are the result of a much more complex situation. Nevertheless there is a certain parallelism between the two. As the culture and political liberties of the ancient world were the product of the city state and its citizen class, so Western culture and freedom has been developed by the privileged or citizen classes of the relatively small-scale societies of the European state-system which included the Western national monarchies, the Italian city states and German principalities. And our problem arises from the difficulty of adapting the cultural ideals and the political institutions that had developed in this restricted field to the new world of large-scale mass states, in the same way that the ancient world was forced to adapt the institutions and ideals of the city state to the cosmopolitan conditions of world empire.

Thus in both cases we see the same tendency of culture to deteriorate in quality as it increases in quantity, and for the cruder and less highly developed political traditions to reassert themselves over the more delicate and civilized ones. The general tendency in the ancient world was the resurgence of the traditions of Oriental despotism against that of Western citizenship, and in the world today we see a similar process in the decline of democracy and the revival of a new type of absolutism in central and eastern Europe which had formerly been ruled by military autocracies or authoritarian monarchies.

If we follow out this analogy the conclusion would seem to be that the cause of democracy is hopeless and that Western Europe is fated to become the prey of totalitarian autocracies which grow progressively bigger and worse. Personally I am not a fatalist, and an analogy of this kind while it does throw some light on the historical situation has not the character of a mechanical law of fatality and determination. Moreover, the divisions in our civilization however exaggerated by racial and nationalist propaganda are far more superficial than those which separated the peoples of the ancient world. The latter was composed of elements which were essentially disparate. The ancient Oriental monarchies, the city states of the Mediterranean and the tribal societies of Western Europe had been forcibly united by the military power of Rome, but they had no common spiritual background and no common origins. They had their roots in different worlds. In the modern world, on the contrary, we have an entirely different situation. For a thousand years the peoples and states of Europe have developed under similar influences and shared a common cultural patrimony. They have all received their education in the school of Christendom, and, however disobedient they have been to its teachings and its discipline, they still bear its imprint and retain a half-conscious memory of their former spiritual unity.

But if this be so, why is not Christianity the rallying point of Western unity? Why does it seem powerless to counteract the forces that are tearing Europe asunder?

The reason is that religion itself is a disunited and therefore disunifying force. Before European civilization was secularized, Christendom was already divided. In fact, the modern liberal secular state emerged as a solution of the problem of religious disunity which had plunged almost all the peoples of Europe into civil war, and the reaction against the enlightenment and the failure of the liberal state have brought us back not to the age of religious unity but to the age of the wars of religion.

Beneath the ideological conflicts which divide the modern world there lie the old theological conflicts which were ignored during the last two centuries of material progress but which nevertheless have left a profound trauma in the European soul. The more we can bring to light these hidden sources of misunderstanding and conflict, the more hope there will be of a spiritual reconciliation which is the only true foundation of international peace and order, so that the problem of the reunion of Christendom has a much closer relation to the cause of world peace than is generally realized.

Here there are three problems to be considered. There is the schism between Eastern and Western Christendom, there is the division between Catholic and Protestant Europe and thirdly there are the internal divisions of Protestantism itself.

The first of these is relatively simple and obvious. The religious division between the East and the West coincides with a very clearly cut cultural division which separates Eastern and Western Europe. The Orthodox Christendom of Russia and the Balkans was for centuries a closed world to the Latin West in which all the streams of thought and social culture and religious tradition ran in a separate channel. For the Orthodox Russian of the later Middle Ages the Christian West did not exist, and after the fall of Byzantium and the Turkish conquest of the Balkans nothing existed save Russia herself, the Third Rome. As the monk Filofei wrote to Ivan III: "Take note, O religious and gracious Tsar, that all Christian kingdoms are merged in thine alone, that two Romes have fallen, but the third stands, and there will be no fourth. Thy Christian kingdom shall not fall to the lot of another."

Thus behind the closed world of the Soviet Republics, with its absolute identification with Communist ideology and its absolute submission to the Communist dictator, there lies the closed world of Orthodox Russia with its absolute identification with the Orthodox Church and its absolute submission to the Orthodox Czar. Berdyaev, to name only one among many, has clearly shown how the one was transformed into the other in consequence of the victorious expansion of Western culture into Russia and the conflict that developed between the military police state of post-Petrine Russia and the old ideal of Holy Russia which was deeply embedded in the popular mind. The tension was not finally resolved until the state itself was captured by the secular Messianism of the revolutionary intelligentsia which thus created the earliest and the most complete form of the new totalitarian absolutism. For we cannot insist too strongly that the totalitarian idea was not Fascist or Italian or German in origin. It was a distinctively Russian reaction which could not have arisen without the centuries of cultural segregation and politico-religious unity which formed the Russian national consciousness.

In Western Christendom, on the other hand, both the religious and the cultural development are infinitely more complex and multiform. Here the religious divisions are of comparatively recent date and throughout a large part of Europe they are confused and indistinct. Our Western civilization is, in fact, characterized by a remarkable lack of religious uniformity, and the problem of religious minorities has been a far more burning question in the past than any question of racial minorities today.

There is, of course, the uniform Latin Catholicism of Italy, Spain, Portugal and South America, and the solid block of Scandinavian Lutheranism, but the countries which have taken the leading part in the development of modern culture—France and Germany, Switzerland and the Low Countries, the United Kingdom and the United States—have also been divided in religion in various degrees. In some cases, as in France, the religious minority barely survived centuries of ostracism and persecution. In Germany and in Switzerland the country was subdivided territorially into a patchwork of rival confessions. While in England, and still more in the United States, the sectarian principle was increasingly dominant, until religion became a personal matter which depended on the free choice of the individual. The problems arising from this state of religious disunion in a society which nevertheless possesses a common cultural tradition have not hitherto been sufficiently appreciated by the historians or the sociologists.

Obviously I cannot attempt here to deal with them all even in the most summary fashion. What I propose to do is to say something about the social consequences of the divergence between the two main religious traditions within the Protestant world, for here we find the seeds of the spiritual conflict which divides Western civilization today, and although the theological divisions were never profound and are now almost ignored, they have had historical consequences of incalculable importance.

Nothing, in fact, is more striking than the way in which Lutheranism and Calvinism in spite of their fundamental theological agreement have produced or helped to produce totally different social attitudes and have become embodied in opposite political traditions. For while Lutheranism almost from the beginning adopted a passive attitude towards the state and accepted a highly conservative and even patriarchal conception of political authority, Calvinism has proved a revolutionary force in European and American history and has provided the moral dynamic element in the great expansion of bourgeois culture from the sixteenth to the nineteenth centuries.

How is this contrast to be explained? To a great extent, no doubt, it is due to accidental circumstances which confined Lutheranism to the static territorial states of Germany and Scandinavia and brought Calvinism into relation with the rising commercial communities of the Netherlands and England. But this is not all. For the contrast is already present in the thought and personality of the two protagonists. Luther's political quietism is not simply the result of his social environment. It springs from the deepest roots of his religious experience. It is clearly shown in the following famous passages which I quote from Troeltsch's *Social Teaching of the Christian Churches,* a book which contains an extraordinary wealth of reference on the whole problem we are discussing.

A child [Luther writes] would understand from these sayings [of our Lord] that it is a Christian law not to resist evil, not to take to the sword, not to defend oneself, not to revenge oneself, but to deliver up one's body and one's possessions, and let anyone take it who will. We indeed have enough in our Lord Himself, who will not leave us, as he had promised, "Suffer, suffer, Cross, cross." This is the Christian's law and there is none other.

If thou sufferest violence or injustice, thou must say that is the government of this world. If thou wilt live in the world that is what thou must expect. Thou wilt never succeed in bringing about that it should happen otherwise. If thou wilt live among the wolves then one must howl with them. Here in this world we are staying in an inn where the Devil is Master and the world is landlady and all kinds of evil passions are servants and these are the enemies and opponents of the Gospel. Thus, if thy money is stolen or thou art injured in thine honour, that is just what thou hast to expect in this house.

On this passage, Brandenburg makes the following comment which is worth quoting:

Nowhere do I find the essential element in Luther's

outlook on the world so clearly expressed as in this illus-
tration. The monk wishes to escape the service of the
devilish landlord by flight, the struggling Church desires
to tear the rule out of the hands of the innkeeper by
external means of authority and to gain control of the
domestics; at first Luther hoped to convert the inhabitants and fill them with the Christian spirit; now, however, he has given up this hope, but in spite of that, he
wants to stay in the terrible house. For he is not there of
his own will, but because he has been placed there by
his God.

Therefore he desires to do his duty here, to let himself
be beaten and ill-treated if it pleases the evil master and
his servants to do so, but he will not stir from the spot
till his Master call him away, and every good hour that
he enjoys he will rejoice in as a special grace.*

Taking these passages (and other similar ones) by
themselves it is easy to interpret Luther's attitude as
an extreme form of Christian pacifism and other-
worldliness, similar to that which we find in some of
the early Quakers. But there is another side to this
thought. In spite of his super-Augustinian opposition
of the Church and the world, Luther never regarded
the State as evil or criticized temporal authority. He
himself said, "I have written about the secular authority as glorious and useful as no teacher has done since
the time of the Apostles excepting possibly St. Augustine."** Still more important is the emphasis that he
lays on the acceptance by the individual of his place

* E. Troeltsch, *The Social Teaching of the Christian Churches
and Groups* (Engl. Transl.) II, pp. 867 f., and E. Brandenburg,
Luthers Anschauung von Staat und Gesellschaft, p. 5.
** *Krieg wider die Tuerken*, BA IV, 1. 441.

in the social order as the divinely ordered means of his sanctification. The words of the English Church catechism "to order myself lowly and reverently to all my betters and to do my duty in that state of life to which it shall please God to call me" is thoroughly Lutheran in spirit. In fact, there is a remarkable resemblance between the old High Church Anglican doctrine of the sacred character of authority—the Divine Right of Kings—and the correlative doctrine of passive obedience on the part of the subject and the conservative patriarchalism of German Lutheranism, though the latter survived to a much later period than the former, and had a more definitely feudal character.

There is, however, another element that is peculiar to Lutheranism and especially to Luther himself. That is the instinctive tendency to aggression and violence which is so characteristic of Luther's polemic writings and which emerges particularly strongly in his writings against the revolting peasants. "One cannot argue reasonably with a rebel but one must answer him with the fist so that his nose bleeds." Or, "It is better that all the peasants should be killed than that the princes and magistrates should perish, for the rustics took the sword without divine authority."

These utterances may perhaps be dismissed as violent expressions of a passionate nature. But there is more to it than that. There is a background of religion, almost of mysticism, to Luther's cult of power. For though he believes that all power comes from God and that the authority of the State rests on the Natural Law and the Divine will, he sees this law not, as St. Thomas did, as the law of reason, but as the mysterious and divine power which rules this present evil world, "the Kingdom of wrath and punishment." "In this kingdom there is nothing but punishment and resistance, judgment and condemnation, in order to force the evil and to protect the good. Therefore also this kingdom possesses and wields the sword."

Consequently he can even go so far as to say: "The hand that wields the secular sword is not a human hand, but the hand of God. It is God not man who hangs and breaks on the wheel, beheads and scourges. It is God who wages war."*

This Lutheran tradition, with its strange dualism of pessimism and faith, other-worldliness and world affirmation, passive quietism and crude acceptance of the reign of force, has been the most powerful force in the formation of the German mind and the German social attitude. It played a considerable part in the development of German idealism. It lies behind Hegel's exaltation of the Prussian state as the supreme expression of Absolute Spirit, and his conception of History as the manifestation of God in time, so that *Welt-Geschichte* and *Welt-Gericht*—world history and world judgment—are the same. Here also we find the same cult of power and force which found its extreme expression among the disciples of Hegel, and inspired Belinsky's famous essay on the Battle of Borodino which caused such heart burnings among the Russian intelligentsia of the '40s. But it had a still greater and far more direct influence on German

* Ob Kriegsleute selig werden koennen. XIX, 626.

political thought, where it fused with the Catholic elements of the Romantic Revival to produce the new Prussian conservatism of F. J. Stahl and Bismarck.

Here Luther's cult of force and his "natural law of irrationalism" becomes transformed into the cult of militarism and of a non-moral or super-moral *Machtpolitik*. Hence Troeltsch sees in the restoration of Prussian German Lutheranism "one of the most important events in social history," during the nineteenth century.

Along with the international Catholic Restoration policy [he writes], which was akin to it and yet so very different from it and with which it is in contact sometimes friendly, sometimes hostile—Lutheranism occupies the key position of the most difficult and pregnant problems affecting the life of Germany, and does its part towards widening the gulf between the forces which support the cause of democracy and progress, a gulf in which all moderate attempts at reconciliation are drowned; for the longing to bridge over this gulf in Germany with a Christian-Social programme was an idealistic and praiseworthy but fleeting and swiftly refuted dream.*

The whole of this tradition and the thought and ideals that it has produced is almost ignored in England and this is in my opinion one of the most profound causes of the conflict and misunderstanding which divide Western civilization today. For behind Western democracy there lies the spiritual world of Calvinism and the Free Churches, which is, as I have

* Troeltsch, *Social Teaching of the Christian Churches* (English transl.), II, p. 576.

said, completely different in its political and social outlook from the world of Lutheranism, and which has had a far greater influence and closer connexion with what we know as Western civilization or even as civilization without further qualification.

This divergence was only fully manifested in the course of centuries, but it was not simply a result of historical circumstance. It had its root in the very origins of the two confessions and in the personality of their founders. At first sight this may seem difficult to maintain. For there is in the teaching of Calvin the same pessimism with regard to human nature and human will, the same other-worldliness and the same exaltation of divine power and even arbitrariness that is to be found in Luther. Nevertheless, all these conceptions were transformed by the intense spirit of moral activism which characterized Calvin and Calvinism. The genius of Calvin was that of an organizer and legislator, severe, logical, and inflexible in purpose, and consequently it was he and not Luther who inspired Protestantism with the will to dominate the world and to change society and culture. Hence though Calvinism has always been regarded as the antithesis of Catholicism to a far greater extent than Lutheranism, it stands much nearer to Catholicism in its conception of the relation of Church and State and in its assertion of the independence and supremacy of the spiritual power. In this respect it carries on the traditions of medieval Catholicism and of the Gregorian movement of reform to an even greater degree than did the Catholicism of the Counter-Reformation itself.

In an age when the Papacy was dependent on the Habsburg monarchies and when Catholics accepted the theories of passive obedience and the divine right of kings, the Calvinists asserted the Divine Right of Presbytery* and declared that "the Church was the foundation of the world" and that it was the duty of kings to "throw down their crowns before her and lick the dust from off her feet."** But these theocratic claims were not hierarchic and impersonal as in the medieval Church, they were based on an intense individualism deriving from the certainty of election and the duty of the individual Christian to co-operate in realizing the divine purpose against a sinful and hostile world. Thus Calvinism is at once aristocratic and democratic; aristocratic in as much as the "saints" were an elect minority chosen from the mass of fallen humanity and infinitely superior to the children of this world; but democratic in that each was directly responsible to God who is no respecter of persons. Calvinism is, in fact, a democracy of saints, elect of God, but also in a sense self-chosen, since it is the conscience of the individual which is the ultimate witness of his election.

It is not, however, in Genevan Calvinism but in English and American Puritanism that these concepts of the Holy Community and the cosmic mission of the saints attain their full expression. For in England the pure Calvinist tradition was united with that of the Anabaptist and the independent sects to produce a

---

* *The Divine Right of Presbytery Asserted.*
** Cartwright. "Replye to an answere" (1573), p. 180 in J. W. Allen, *Political Thought in the Sixteenth Century*, p. 221 (1928).

new movement which is political as well as religious and which marks the first appearance of genuine democracy in the modern world. And in this revolutionary attempt to transform the English State into a Holy Community, "to build Jerusalem in England's green and pleasant land," the Calvinist conception of the democratic aristocracy of the saints provided the inspiration and the driving force.

I will illustrate this from the sermon which Thomas Goodwin, one of the most orthodox Calvinists among the Independent leaders, preached before the House of Commons in February, 1645.

The theme of his sermon was "The Great Interest of States and Kingdoms" and his conclusion is *The Saints of England are the Interest of England.*

This is our great security; and it is the more special interest of the kingdom in which we live, the *magna charta* of it. And when I say saints, I mean no one party of men. Do we not know that the new creature is found in circumcision and uncircumcision and as eminent in the one as in the other? and it were the highest sacrilege in the world to engross that title of saints and the godly party to any one. Characters of saints I need not give you; it hath been the main subject of the preaching in this kingdom for these forty years and upwards to describe them to you and to distinguish men from men.

As there are multitudes of people, called and chosen ones, in this kingdom, so you honourable and worthy senators are the called and chosen out of all these to this great work. . . . Consider the trust God hath committed to you. You have the richest treasury that I know God hath above ground elsewhere on earth. The saints of England are the interest of England. Write this upon

your walls to have it in your eye in all your consulta-
tions, never to swerve from it for any other interest what-
soever. And have respect to the saints and to the whole
lump of them. If you will maintain your interest whole
and entire, have regard to the saints small and great.

It was, however, not in Parliament but in the
Army that the aristo-democracy of the saints found
its most complete expression. It is the dominant note
of the Army Debates at Putney in 1647, when the
delegates of the regiments took matters into their own
hands and stood forward as the representatives of the
people and the saints against both King and Parliament. For the Army and Cromwell himself regarded
themselves as the executive arm of the Holy Community, divinely commissioned by their special calling
to maintain the rights of God and the people. The
spirit that animated them finds a remarkable expression in the declaration that was issued from a camp
at Musselburgh during the Scotch campaign of 1650:

At the beginning of the great and wonderful workings
of God in these two nations of England and Scotland
we the under-officers and soldiers of the English Army
now in Scotland were most of us (if not all) men of
private callings and not at all interested in matters of
public and state affairs. But upon the beginning of the
civil war we found our hearts extraordinarily stirred up
by the Lord to assist the Parliament against the King,
being abundantly satisfied in our hearts and consciences
that we were called forth by the Lord to be instrumental
to bring about that which was our continual prayer to
God, viz. the destruction of Antichrist and the deliverance of His Church and people. And upon this simple

account we engaged, not knowing the deep policies of worldly statesmen, and have ever since hazarded our lives in the high places of the field, where we have seen the wonders of the Lord, against all the opposers of this work of Jesus Christ Whom we have all along seen going with us and making our way plain before us. . . .

And here give us leave to tell you that we are persuaded we are poor unworthy instruments in God's hand, to break His enemies and to preserve His people. . . . We desire it may be known unto you, our brethren of Scotland, that we are not soldiers of fortune, we are not merely the servants of men; we have not only proclaimed Jesus Christ, the King of Saints, to be our King by profession but desire to submit to Him upon His own terms and to admit Him to the exercise of His royal authority in our hearts and to follow Him withersoever He goeth. He having of His own good will entered into a covenant of Grace with His poor saints.*

This translation of the conception of the Holy Community from an ecclesiastical ideal to a principle of revolutionary political action was not confined to the sectarian extremists such as the Baptists and Fifth Monarchy men: it was accepted by the leading Independent divines such as the two Goodwins, by intellectuals like Vane and Milton and by the leaders of the Army itself, Cromwell and Ireton. John Goodwin, the great apostle of Toleration, even goes so far as to compare the "Christianly heroic" spirit of the Army with the example of "the Lord Jesus Christ, Blessed for ever, who went down into the chambers of death

* A Declaration of the English Army now in Scotland from the leaguer at Muscleborough, 1 August, 1654. In Woodhouse, *Puritanism and Liberty,* pp. 474-6.

from thence to bring up with him a lost world."*
And, in fact, it does mark the beginning of a new
world, for, as Troeltsch points out, the great experiment of the Cromwellian Commonwealth, short-lived
though it was, by the momentum of its religious impulse opened the way for a new type of civilization
based on the freedom of the person and of conscience
as rights conferred absolutely by God and Nature.
The connexion is seen most clearly in America where
the Congregationalist Calvinism of New England
which was a parallel development to the Independent
Puritanism of old England, developing from the same
roots in a different environment, leads on directly to
the assertion of the Rights of Man in the constitutions
of the North American States and to the rise of political democracy. But it also inspired the rise of the
new bourgeois liberal culture in England, though
here the development is complicated by the catastrophic collapse of the Cromwellian experiment and
the partial secularization of its ideals in Locke and
the second English Revolution.

Taking a broad view, therefore, it is impossible to
deny the importance of the Calvinist Free-Church
tradition in the development of Anglo-Saxon liberal
democracy, so that (as Troeltsch has said) the difference between the political ideals of a Gladstone or an
Abraham Lincoln, and those of Stahl and Bismarck,
mark the great differences between the Continental
Lutheran and the Anglo-Saxon world of thought,
which was determined or influenced by Calvinism

* *Might and Right Well Met,* quoted in Woodhouse, *op. cit.,*
p. 220.

and the Free Churches. Behind the latter there lies
the ideal of the Holy Community, secularized in so
far as it is now applied to great civilized nations but
still preserving its moral activism and its will to dominate and reform the world. Thus the modern Western
belief in progress, in the rights of man and the duty
of conforming political action to moral ideals, whatever they may owe to other influences, derive ultimately from the moral ideals of Puritanism and its
faith in the possibility of the realization of the Holy
Community on earth by the efforts of the elect. While
the German combination of realism and mysticism,
of external discipline and internal anarchy, which is
so alien to our way of thought, has its roots in the
Lutheran world view with its conception of humanity
as the passive instrument of the mighty forces of irrational nature and irresistible grace.

Thus the two main types of Protestantism represent not only two different ideas of the Church and of
its relation to the world, but also two opposite concepts of Natural Law. Luther's conception of the
Natural Law, in so far as it affects the state, is a real-
istic recognition of the concrete order of society as
produced by Providence in the course of history; or
to use the expression of Kaufmann and Troeltsch, it
is the Natural Law of irrationalism.* Calvin, on the
other hand, regarded the Natural Law in the traditional way as identical with the moral law, as the
norm to which all social and individual behaviour
must conform and which rests, in the last resort, on

* Cf. Troeltsch II. p. 616.

the will of God, as revealed to man's reason and conscience.

And this opposition still holds good today, in spite
of the centuries of secularization which have transformed European culture. For the conflict between
Western democracy and Nazi Germany is at the bottom a conflict between two opposite conceptions of
Natural Law and consequently of public morality.
To the German, the Anglo-Saxon appeal to morality
in international politics and their assertion of ethical
humanitarian ideals appear unreal, hypocritical and
a cloak for selfish imperialism. While to us, the German exaltation of power for its own sake, the glorifi-
cation of war, the disregard of the rights of the individual and contempt of humanitarian ideals appear
irrational, immoral and anti-Christian. Where the
Christian tradition still remains alive, even if it is
not intact, the possibility of understanding remains,
as we see in the case of Bismarck and his friend, that
typical Anglo-Saxon, J. L. Motley. But when Christianity disappears, the gulf becomes unfathomable,
as it is today between the Nazi neo-paganism and the
secularized liberalism or Liberal Socialism of the
Anglo-Saxon world.

Hitherto, however, we have said nothing of the religious tradition which underlies the whole development of Western culture and which has contributed
more than any other factor to the formation of its
spiritual and social unity. Catholicism was the matrix
out of which the two religious traditions of which we
have been speaking emerged, and from the Protestant
point of view history would have been much simpler

if Catholicism had ceased to exist with the coming of
the Reformation. In fact, however, Catholicism not
only exists, but co-exists with Protestantism, so that
there is today no cultural area which is exclusively and
homogeneously Protestant. And as Catholicism cuts
across the national political and cultural frontiers, so
also is it with the ideological differences which we
have been discussing.

For on the one hand the Catholic political tradition
in the narrower sense, i.e., the historic type of the
Catholic state, agrees with the Lutheran-Continental
tradition in its authoritarianism, its conservative traditionalism and its acceptance of a strict corporative
order of society. On the other hand, it stands far
closer to the Western-Calvinist tradition in its view
of the relation of the Church to the state, in the primacy of the spiritual power, above all in its conception of Natural Law. The Calvinist idea of Natural
Law is fundamentally identical with that of Catholic
philosophy, except that the latter puts a stronger emphasis on its rational character, as against the Calvinist voluntarism. And in the development of political
thought in the sixteenth century there is a curious parallelism between the political doctrine of the Jesuits,
Molina, Mariana and Suarez, and that of the French
Huguenot publicists.

Similarly with regard to the question of the sovereignty of the people as against the divine right of
kings: the Calvinist protest which was fully developed in Scotland and France rather than at Geneva is
directly connected with the teaching of later scholas-
ticism through John Major who was the teacher both

of Knox and Buchanan, and whose influence may be
traced on Huguenot thought as, for example, in the
Vindiciae contra Tyrannos.

These common elements explain the fact that in
later periods there was a process of mutual influence
and cross fertilization between the political thought
of the Western Protestant and Catholic societies so
that modern liberal democracy has not been confined
to one or the other or derived exclusively from one
or the other, since each possessed a common tradition
of Natural Law on which the Rights of Man could
be based. Yet at the same time Catholicism also had
its links with the Lutheran world, and this common
element emerged in the political thought of the Restoration, which was due to the interaction of German and Catholic elements under the influence of
the Romantic movement of the early nineteenth century.

Today with the decline of liberal democracy it is
natural that the traditions of political authoritarianism and traditionalism in Catholic countries should
reassert themselves, but the principles of Natural Law
are so deeply implanted in the Catholic tradition that
they can never be ignored. It has, in fact, been the
foremost concern of the Papacy from the time of Leo
XIII to recall these principles to the mind of the
modern world, and the present Pope in his Encyclical
on the war expressly singled out the modern denial
or neglect of the Natural Law as the profound source
from which all the characteristic evils of the modern
state derive their origin. Thus the belief in the ethical
basis of social and political life which was the original

inspiration of Western democracy finds its justification in the teaching of the Catholic Church and the
tradition of Western Christendom. It is opposed today by the unethical natural law of race and class and
the Machiavellian realism which makes power the
supreme political value and which does not shrink
from the blackest treachery or the most brutal cruelty
to gain its ends.

The centre of these hostile forces is to be found in
the states of Central and Eastern Europe which, in
spite of their great cultural achievements, have been
relatively backward in political development and
lacked the political ethos which the Western peoples
acquired through their intensive training in self-
government. They are spreading rapidly throughout
the modern world owing to the deterioration of cultural standards which accompanies the development
of mass civilization, for in politics, as in economics,
the baser currency tends to drive out the good. And
this is above all the case in time of war, when all the
power and resources of the modern state are organized
for human destruction. For in war the temptation to
"howl with the wolves" is often overwhelmingly
strong. Nevertheless the end of war from the Christian standpoint is not the release of the forces of disorder but the mastering of them by a violent effort of
disciplined will. The only thing that makes the evils
of war bearable is the hope of Peace—not merely the
negative peace of a cessation of hostilities but the true
peace of justice and freedom. The Western mind cannot permanently acquiesce in the idea of a state of
society without justice or freedom, a state which, as

St. Augustine says, is nothing but wholesale robbery. Western civilization, in spite of all its failures, has been acutely conscious of the value of social justice: in fact, the driving force behind the development of Western democracy has been the will to create a society which was not merely the instrument of power but which rested on moral foundations, which protected the rights of the weak against the privileges of the strong and the freedom of the individual against the unlimited authority of the state itself. This is why the modern denial of the principles of natural law is more fatal to the democratic state that was founded upon them than it is to the authoritarian type of state which regarded power as its own justification. And as the loss of the ethical basis of political and international life is the main cause of the disintegration of Western culture, the only way to reintegration is that pointed out by Pius XII in his address to the Cardinals on Christmas Eve 1939, when he proclaimed a new crusade to "lead the nations back from the broken cisterns of material and selfish interests to the living fountain of divine justice."

4

The Failure of Liberalism

DURING the last twenty years we have seen the collapse of constitutional government throughout Europe, and with it the loss of personal freedom and economic freedom and intellectual freedom—in fact all the liberties which the nineteenth century believed had been won or were being won as a permanent possession for humanity. Are we to believe that these liberties were a sham and proved their worthlessness as soon as they were won? Or were they so bound up with the social and economic circumstances of the last century that they were necessarily transcended by the new developments of twentieth-century culture? Or finally have they been betrayed by the liberals themselves? And is their defeat due to lack of faith in principles that are eternally valid?

There is something to be said for each of these explanations which one may describe respectively as Fascist, Marxist, and Democratic. The collapse of constitutional government and the renaissance of despotism are far too real and too momentous to be explained superficially. They amount to a change in the whole spirit of our civilization which could not have occurred unless the process of disintegration had been a far-reaching and many-sided one.

The failure to recognize this on the part of Liberals

during the last two or three generations is largely responsible for the gravity of the present situation. Before we can look forward to the future, we must recognize the mistakes of the past and understand the real nature of the forces that are transforming the modern world.

The great obstacle that stands in the way of this clarification of the issues is the confusion of thought which has created such misunderstanding of the true nature of liberalism alike among its supporters and its opponents. It is essential to define our terms; for there is no word—not even democracy—that has been used so loosely to cover such a variety of divergent elements. The term conservatism is so closely associated with party politics that it does not give occasion to anything like the same degree of confusion, whereas liberalism has always had an ideological character that carries it far beyond the field of party politics. For example when Professor Laski writes the history of the Rise of European Liberalism he is writing the history of a philosophy or a *Weltanschauung*, and the whole history of Liberalism as an English political movement lies outside the scope of his book which, I think, ends with the French Revolution. Hence we must distinguish between liberalism as a political party, liberalism as an ideology, and liberalism as a tradition.

The roots of the liberal *tradition* lie so deep in English and American history that they are almost inseparable, while the liberal *ideology* owes almost as much to France as it does to England. Liberalism as a *party name*, on the other hand, had its origins in

Spain and had spread throughout the greater part of Europe and South America before being officially adopted in this country. Used in this sense liberalism is of course limited to a particular political and social environment. In fact there are as many liberalisms as there are liberal parties so that what is liberalism in one country may be conservatism in another and revolution in a third. Thus in England political liberalism in the narrower sense took shape in the middle decades of the nineteenth century under the leadership of Cobden and Bright and Gladstone in close relation with the Free Trade movement and with Protestant nonconformity. The identification of economic interest and religious idealism which resulted from the combination of these two influences may seem naïve to the modern post-Marxian age, but it was of the very essence of the movement. When, for example, Cobden wrote, "We advocate nothing but what is agreeable to the highest behests of Christianity—to buy in the cheapest market and to sell in the dearest," he was both completely sincere and entirely representative of the spirit of utilitarian pietism which inspired English liberalism in its classical period.

French liberalism, on the other hand, had a far more intellectual and doctrinaire character. It was in the main the creation of the philosophers and men and women of letters who were in opposition to Napoleon and whom he described in Fascist style as "Twelve or fifteen metaphysicians who ought to be thrown into the water." Thus French liberalism from the first had a far more vivid sense of the danger of despotism than English and since it had seen France pass from the despotism of the *ancien régime* to the revolutionary totalitarianism of the Jacobins and then to the military dictatorship of Napoleon, it realized that this danger was not confined to one political extreme. Hence the great French liberals like Benjamin Constant, Maine de Biran, Royer-Collard and de Tocqueville are in a sense more modern and certainly more conscious of the fundamental issues of politics than the English liberals who were their successors in time. Nevertheless they were better philosophers than politicians. They lacked the firmly established tradition of political and social liberty which England possessed, and consequently they built too high for their foundation so that again and again the whole political edifice crumbled under the shock of revolution.

In the case of the third country I have mentioned, Spain, liberalism was even farther removed from the political and cultural traditions of the nation than it was in France. Spanish liberalism was an imported product which at certain periods enjoyed all the popularity that a foreign fashion in ideas often acquires. And for the same reason it aroused the native fanaticism of the Spanish character against it. And this situation was rendered even more acute by the identification of the old order in Spain with the Church and by the theocratic character which the Spanish monarchy had acquired by its relation to the Inquisition. Thus in Spain and in South America alike liberalism was forced into the position of a rival religion and this identification of liberalism with anticlericalism has not only had a permanent effect on Spanish history but has had its repercussion on Catholics elsewhere, above all in Southern Italy where the origins of liberalism were associated with the Spanish movement, as opposed to Lombardy and Tuscany where Italian liberalism had a much closer affinity to the French type.

I have made this brief survey of some of the main types of European liberalism, because it is useless to discuss liberalism in the abstract unless one bears in mind the concrete social and historical background of the different forms of liberalism. In England, for example, when the doctrine of *laissez faire* and the cult of economic individualism became discredited there was a tendency for liberalism to become an abstract ideal somewhat insecurely attached to a party machine. And when the machine broke down, as it did in most countries long before the rise of Fascism, this abstract idealism provided no solid basis for any new political activity.

Are we to conclude as Dr. Mannheim does in his *Man and Society* that "from the wreckage of Liberalism nothing can be saved but its values"? It would certainly be the case if we regard Liberalism as inseparable from the old economic individualism or explain it, as Professor Laski does, as "the by-product of the effort of the middle classes to win their place in the sun." But the liberal ideology is much more than that and the tradition out of which that ideology arose is greater still. For this tradition has been central to Western civilization and in spite of the defeats and disillusions of the last thirty years it is still a living force in the world today. I admit that liberalism is not an altogether satisfactory name to give it, for it means narrowing it down to one particular manifestation of it. On the other hand the term democracy which is in general use today is in some respects even less satisfactory, since equalitarian democracy can so easily be used (and has in fact so often been used) as the instrument of mass despotism which is diametrically opposed to the liberal principle, alike in its narrower and its more universal sense.

For it is freedom and not equality that has been the inspiration of Western culture and the whole history of Western man has been a long quest for freedom. Western civilization has never been a geographical or racial unity. It was born on the shores of the Aegean between the barbarism of continental Europe and the civilized despotism of Asia in that new world of tiny city states which was the source of a new way of living and new conceptions of law and citizenship. But this freedom was no lawless individualism like that of the barbarian. It was the fruit of an intensive effort of social discipline and organization. As Herodotus says in the speech that he puts into the mouth of the exiled Spartan king at the Persian court, "For though the Greeks are freemen they are not free in every respect. Law is the master they own, and this master they fear more than thy subjects fear thee."

This new conception of life was put to the test in the great war in which the free Greek cities withstood the mass attack of Asiatic despotism and emerged triumphant. And in the following centuries the Hellenic world proved for the first time and for all time what the human spirit was capable of when it was set free from slavery to the rule of force. How this tradition of Western civilization survived the decline of the city state and the loss of its political freedom has always been the greatest of historical problems. The answer of the old school of liberal historians was that it did not survive:—that the light of classical civilization was extinguished in the night of the Dark Ages and was reborn miraculously at the Renaissance which was the starting point of the new period of progress and enlightenment. The other view which I myself hold is that the ancient world saved its soul by its conversion to Christianity and that the tradition of its culture lived on in Western Christendom. The loss of political freedom in the ancient world was in fact counterbalanced by the revelation of a new spiritual freedom; so when the earthly city was enslaved men acquired faith in the existence of a spiritual city "which is free and the mother of us all." And as the first epoch in the history of freedom is marked by the rise of the free Greek cities and their struggle with Persia, the second is marked by the rise of the Christian Church and its struggle with the Roman Empire which had lost the ideals of citizenship and political freedom and was rapidly becoming a vast servile state like those of the ancient East. The battle was fought out under the shadow of the executioners' rods and axes in praetoria and amphitheatres and concentration camps from Germany to Africa and from Spain to Armenia, and its heroes were the martyrs—Martyrum candidatus exercitus. Henceforward wherever the Christian faith was preached not only in Europe but from one end of the world to the other, from Japan and Annam to Canada, the names of the men who bore witness with their blood to truth and spiritual freedom have been held in honour and it is only today with the rise of the new totalitarian challenge to Christian values that the principle of martyrdom and *the honour of the martyrs* has been called in question.

The dynamic force of this spiritual ideal put new life into the dying civilization of the ancient world and gave Latin Christendom the power to incorporate the northern barbarians in the new synthesis of Western medieval civilization. Here again the principle of freedom was central to the new cultural development, hard as it may be for the modern democrat to recognize anything in common between his ideals and those of the Catholic feudal world. Nevertheless the old liberals realized it half consciously by their idealization of Magna Charta and of the medieval communal and constitutional movement. It is true that what the Middle Ages called liberties were very different from the liberty of the Declaration of Independence and still more from that of the French Revolution. Nevertheless, at the roots of the development of Western freedom and Western democracy there lies the medieval idea that men possess rights even against the state and that society is not a totalitarian political unit but a community made up of a complex variety of social organisms, each possessing an autonomous life and its own free institutions.

It was in England in the seventeenth century that the Christian ideal of spiritual freedom and the medieval tradition of political liberties came together to produce the new liberal ideology which was the main inspiration of Western civilization for more than two centuries and out of which political liberalism in the strict sense finally developed. The failure of liberalism in the course of the last century has been due above all to the failure of the liberal parties to give adequate expression to this ideology and to the still deeper social tradition that lies behind it. The liberal movement in the wider sense transformed the world by an immense liberation of human energies, but liberalism in the narrower sense proved incapable of guiding the forces that it had released. It became a negative and defensive creed which from the socialist standpoint represented nothing more than class interest. Nevertheless the socialist criticism of liberalism was at least in its early form a product of liberal ideology. It was the extension to a wider class of the ideal which had been at first limited to the politically conscious minority. The fundamental appeal of socialism lay in its assertion of real social rights against abstract political ones. It is a recall to the same principle which had inspired the forerunners of English liberalism and which was stated so admirably by one of the spokesmen of Cromwell's army when he declared "The poorest he that is in England hath a life to live as the richest he."*

This assertion of the right of every man to live a full human life is the essence of socialism, and thus, so far from being in opposition to the liberal tra-

* Col. Rainborough speaking against Ireton at Putney, Oct. 29, 1647.

dition it is an extension of that tradition from the sphere of law and politics to economics and culture. Yet it is impossible to ignore the existence of an anti-liberal element in socialism which has contributed more than any other single factor to the breakdown of freedom in the modern world. For continental social-ism, as represented above all by Karl Marx, is respon-sible not only for the discrediting of the liberal ideol-ogy but for the totalitarian challenge to liberty under the shadow of which we are living today. The revolutionary dictatorship of the proletariat, the use of the power of the state as a weapon to destroy every social element which is opposed to the interests of the dominant class, the substitution of the mass for the individual as the centre of all cultural and moral values—all these principles which lie at the root of the totalitarian state are derived from Marxism and revolutionary socialism. For when once the liberal tradition has been abandoned, the rival forces of totalitarianism rapidly lose their ideological masks and become merely different ways of doing the same thing: that thing being the destruction of freedom and the sacrifice of human life—whether it is the life of rich or poor, bourgeois or proletarian—to the cult of mass power.

Is it possible on the one hand to recover the human and liberal values in socialism from the totalitarian forces that have overcome them and on the other hand to free the liberal tradition itself from its asso-ciation with the narrow economic individualism of the last century? These are the questions that we have to solve, if Democracy is to adapt itself to the changed world of the mid-twentieth century as well as or better than the totalitarian ideologies. The latter, after all, spring from a different soil from ours. They are systems by which societies that have been disciplined for centuries by the traditions of theocratic autocracy or military monarchy have adapted themselves to the new world. Such societies can be revolutionized by a determined minority more easily and rapidly than any democratic society. But that is a source of weakness as well as of strength. The imposing façade of totalitarian unity may conceal the internal weakness of the structure or impose a strain which its social foundations are incapable of supporting.

Moreover the external successes of such movements do nothing to diminish the dangers that confront the modern state as soon as it abandons the political traditions that have hitherto guided Western civilization. The terrifying thing is not the revolutionary violence of the first years of the Russian Revolution or the putsch of 1933 in Germany. It is not the reign of the secret police and the cruelty and treachery that accompany it. It is that there is no limit to the regressive movement: that in a few years a society can pass from a high revolutionary idealism to a state of organized inhumanity which plans the liquidation of classes, the transplantation of populations and the destruction of whole peoples as ruthlessly as the ancient Assyrians or the medieval Tartars. This new barbarism is, in fact, worse than that of the past in that it is inspired not by the naïve cruelty of a simple warrior society but by the perverted science of a corrupt civilization.

But though this barbarism is already upon us, it is largely unconscious and involuntary, and it is not welcomed or openly approved even by those peoples which have contributed most to its onset. Hence the democratic nations in their resistance to this progress to the abyss can rely not only on the support of those who are still faithful to the spiritual traditions of Western civilization, but also to some extent on the secret sympathy of the totalitarian peoples themselves.

The idea of freedom is practically universal, and there is no people, however lacking in political capacity or experience, that is entirely insensitive to its appeal. Where they differ is in the quality of the freedom that they prize most highly and in their power of achieving it against the hostile forces of nature and circumstance. Human life has always been bound by the ultimate necessities of labour and conflict and death, so that many men in every age have been forced to surrender all the other liberties they prize for the bare right to live at all. The essence of civilization consists in the limitation of this empire of necessity and the widening of the sphere of freedom, but in the past there has been so much inequality in the distribution of social gains as to give some colour to Rousseau's criticism of civilization. It was only in the nineteenth century that the advance of science and the growth of man's control over nature made it possible to push back the frontiers of necessity to a point which would have seemed incredible to the thinkers of the past, so that freedom and the opportunity to live the good life need no longer be the privilege of a minority but could become the birthright of every human being.

But the liberal optimism which inspired the nineteenth century expansion of democracy has ended in disillusionment. The new forces that have been generated by science and industry are so gigantic that they seem to dwarf humanity and require giants to control them. Hence the conflict we see today between a liberalism which abandoned the traditional social control in an access of premature optimism and the new collectivism which sacrifices political and social liberty to the ideal of a total organization of society in the interest of efficiency and mass power.

The old liberalism with all its shortcomings had its roots deep in the soil of Western and Christian culture. As Madame de Staël once wrote, "In France liberty is ancient, it is despotism that is modern." But the new collectivism is out of line with the whole Western development. It has more community with the oriental monarchies—with Persia and Assyria and Egypt, with the spirit that inspired the building of the Pyramids and the Great Wall of China.

It is easy to understand the appeal of this spirit to a people like the Russians who have been moulded for centuries by the theocratic ideals of Orthodoxy and Czarism. It is even possible to reconcile it with one side of the German and Central European tradition. But for Western civilization as a whole the victory of such a spirit means death, because it is the denial and destruction of the spiritual principles by which the West has lived. The great tradition of Western civilization has endured so long and survived so many crises that we may believe it is too strong to be destroyed by the new totalitarian enemy. But it cannot be saved by economic and military means alone. As I have said, the crisis would never have arisen if the spiritual forces of Western culture had not been divided and disintegrated. Thus the need transcends politics and demands nothing less than a spiritual re-orientation of Western society and a recall to the essential values which it must preserve at all costs in spite of the revolutionary changes which have destroyed the economic foundations of the old liberal individualism. It is an immense task which demands the co-operation of all the living forces in our culture, in a sustained effort of social and intellectual reorganization. In this work, it seems to me, liberalism occupies a key position, because it is the only political force in Europe which is identified with the cause of freedom and which cannot abandon that cause without ceasing to exist. Socialism, Conservatism and Nationalism are none of them immune to totalitarian influences, whether by propaganda or by a power of internal assimilation. They can assume totalitarian forms without a conscious betrayal of their principles. Even Democracy does not stand in a very firm position since it is always easy for a mass dictatorship to use democratic slogans, especially at the present moment when the leaders of the attack on freedom are not hereditary monarchs or aristocrats but demagogues in the strict sense—perhaps the greatest demagogues that the world has ever known.

But though it is impossible to exaggerate the value

of the liberal tradition in Western culture and the importance of a liberal renaissance it is useless to look for a solution to the revival of the old liberal parties and their recapture of power by the old political methods. The whole situation has changed so fundamentally that we are today faced by the problems that lie outside the scope of politics in the old sense. The new style of totalitarian party dictatorships against which we are fighting attempts to solve these problems and that is the reason for its power. But it does so by a brutal simplification of the issues which sacrifices all the higher values of culture for the sake of immediate material success. It is an attempt to find a short essential cut, and like most such attempts it has only succeeded in losing the way. The task is to bring Western civilization back to the right road. But this cannot be accomplished by the old programmes or political coalitions. It can only be done by the free co-operation of all those who recognize their inherence in the common spiritual tradition of Western civilization and the necessity of creating an organic communion between the scattered and disorganized elements of freedom which still exist though they are politically divided and almost powerless. Such an ideal may seem vague and utopian, but history shows that though permanent elements in a culture like the liberal tradition in Europe may be temporarily submerged or forcibly suppressed they inevitably reassert themselves sooner or later often in a new and unexpected way. The essential thing is to adjust our thought to the new conditions; to see what is living and what is dead in the Western tradition; and to realize that the immense new powers that man has acquired during the last half century can be used in the service of freedom just as easily as they have been used to destroy it.

5

The Failure of the League of Nations

1. The Breakdown of the League

For a thousand years Christian Europe has existed as a true supernational society—a society that was intensely conscious of its community of culture in spite of the continual wars and internal divisions that made up its history. It resembled the unity of the Hellenic world which stood out against the non-Hellenic world as a society of free peoples against the despotisms of the East and as the civilized world—the world of "the good life"—against the world of barbarians.

Today this is no longer so. Europe has lost her unity and the consciousness of the spiritual mission. There is no longer any clear line of division between Christian and non-Christian peoples, and with the disappearance of her Christian consciousness, Europe has begun to doubt her own existence. Each in its own way, modern nationalism and modern internationalism alike have ignored the existence of a European culture and a European society of nations, and have attempted to build a new world on different foundations.

The last war marked the breakdown of the European State-system which goes back to the Treaty of Westphalia in the seventeenth century and which had managed to adapt itself, after a fashion, to the development of Nationalism and democracy during the nineteenth century. But the fall of the three great European monarchies in 1917-18 destroyed the framework of the old State-system and obliged the peacemakers of Versailles to undertake a reorganization of international life more fundamental than anything that had been attempted at any previous period.

They did not restrict themselves to the reorganization of Europe, they attempted to create an international order based on general principles that embraced the whole world. The League of Nations and the Treaty of Versailles with which it was inseparably bound up were the product, on the one hand, of the Liberal idealism of Anglo-Saxon democracy as represented by President Wilson, and on the other of the Nationalist realism of the European victors as represented by M. Clemenceau. While they were hammering out a compromise, new forces were being unleashed on Eastern and Central Europe which were destined to ruin the new edifice of international order before it was fully achieved.

For the League was conceived entirely in the spirit of Anglo-Saxon Liberal democracy, while the world which it aspired to organize was a world that was already far removed from that spiritual tradition and was being carried still further from it by the catastrophic events of war and revolution and economic disaster.

Thus the new international order of Versailles and

Geneva was doomed to failure from the beginning since every year and every fresh political and economic crisis made the contradiction between nineteenth-century ideals and twentieth-century realities more palpable and obvious. Nevertheless the ends for which the League of Nations existed—the preservation of peace and the achievement of international order—remained vital to the existence of our civilization, and each fresh reverse to the League policy has only rendered the need for peace and order more pressing than before. Thus it is of vital importance to distinguish between what is living and what is dead in the ideals of the League of Nations, and to save the cause of international peace and order from being identified with the narrower and, so to speak, more sectarian aspects of modern internationalism.

Under the existing circumstances the tendency has been for idealists to rally to the cause of the League of Nations, so that the League of Nations Union became an idealistic crusade which mobilized all the forces of humanitarian sentiment and moral indignation which are so powerful in the Anglo-Saxon Protestant world, against the war-mongers and dictators who represent the forces of darkness and reaction.

But since the League of Nations was by its origin not a purely ideal construction but an historical creation, based on a definite alignment of political forces, the tendency of opposition to the League also appealed to a kind of idealism which looked on the League as the embodiment of the dark forces of international finance and Western Imperialism. It appealed to the suppressed forces of the nations and classes, whose just rights had been sacrificed by the post-war settlement, to revolt against the international order of Versailles and Geneva.

Now the most paradoxical feature of this situation is the fact that both groups of idealists grounded their appeals on the same principle—the principle of national self-determination; and consequently the controversy over the League of Nations has never been a straight fight between nationalists and internationalists, as the controversy over the Holy Alliance had been a century earlier. Even the extreme form of ultra-nationalism and racialism which has now become identified with the anti-League policy was not originally characteristic of it, for the great Powers which stood out of the League from the beginning, the U.S.A. and the U.S.S.R., were, both of them, markedly anti-racialist, and one of them—Soviet Russia—claimed to be more genuinely international in policy and ideals than the League of Nations itself.

Hence the League of Nations was from the beginning neither wholly Nationalist nor consistently internationalist; it was neither purely idealist nor merely realist. It was an almost complete parallel to the Holy Alliance—that is to say, it was a league of States which existed primarily to preserve the international settlement that had been established as a result of their victory over a military imperialism, and secondarily to establish an international order based on the law of treaties which would secure peace by applying sanctions against any State which attempted to change the *status quo* by force of arms.

Thus it was only to be expected that the break-

down of the Versailles settlement should have been
followed by the breakdown of the League of Nations,
and if the latter is to survive and to serve the wider
ends for which it stands in the eyes of its supporters,
it is necessary to restore it on a wider basis which
corresponds to the realities of the new situation.

The founders of the League of Nations failed to
take account of the new tendencies in international
life which found no place in the optimistic philosophy of Liberal democracy, but which explain the
existing state of world tension and international hostility, though they do not absolve the nations and
their leaders of responsibility for their political acts.
The fact is that the modern world is being driven
along at the same time in two opposite directions.
On the one hand the nations are being brought into
closer contact by the advance of scientific and technical achievement; the limits of space and time that
held them asunder are being contracted or abolished,
and the world has become physically one as never
before. On the other hand, the nations are being
separated from one another by a process of intensive
organization which weakens the spiritual links that
bound men together irrespective of political frontiers and concentrates the whole energy of society
on the attainment of a collective purpose, so as inevitably to cause a collision with the collective will of
other societies.

What makes the danger of war so great today is
not that men are more warlike than in the past, but
that they are more highly organized. War is no longer
the pastime of kings and the trade of professional

armies, it is the death-grapple of huge impersonal mass Powers which have ground out the whole life of the whole population in the wheels of their social mechanism.

The growth of these monstrous organisms is the dominant feature in the modern political system, and they are irreconcilable alike with the old European State system and with the tradition of Liberal democracy that inspired the League of Nations.

2. *The Nation-State and European Unity*

The tragedy of the breakdown of the League of Nations was not simply the result of the unscrupulous greed of the men of power; it was due above all, as I pointed out before, to the conflict and confusion between the two rival idealisms of Nationalism and Liberal democracy which have been the two great motives of political change in the modern world.

In theory, President Wilson gave full recognition to the principle of nationality by basing the League on national self-determination and the sovereignty of the Nation-State. But he failed to realize the strength of the collective passions that underlie these formulas and the difficulty of applying the latter to States like the Habsburg monarchy, which had been created on dynastic and religious principles.

Hence, although the peacemakers of Versailles attempted to base their territorial changes on the principle of national self-determination, they were quite unable to solve the problem of minorities, or even to incorporate the Wilsonian principles themselves in the Covenant of the League. The League

of Nations was, in fact, from the beginning nothing
else but a league of States, and membership of the
League was based entirely on the fact of political
sovereignty without any reference to the national
character of the societies in question.

This is not a mere question of names. It involves
the very essence of the problem of international
order. For the Nations are permanent factors which
remain whether they are given juridical recognition
or not; whereas States, as we have only too much
reason to realize of late years, can change their form
and be multiplied or diminished by wars and revolutions with or without justice or the will of the
peoples concerned. A period like that of the Napoleonic Wars witnessed a wholesale massacre of States,
some of which disappeared for ever, while others
reappeared in a new form when the storm had passed.
Thus a League of Nations created in the year 1800
would have been entirely different in composition
and numbers to the one that actually arose after the
fall of Napoleon. And the transitory character of
these political formations shows that any order that
is based upon them as ultimate Sovereign Powers
must necessarily be impermanent and lacking in
world authority. In Italy, for example, the number
of States that possessed *de facto* sovereignty only
strengthened the case of the partisans of national
unity, although at the same time it rendered the
task of achieving unity by international (or rather,
inter-State) agreement impossibly difficult.

Thus the greatest single cause of the breakdown
of internationalism both in theory and practice has

been the failure to recognize the artificial and unstable character of the political unit on which all our schemes for international organization rest. The word *State* simply signifies an independent political organization, and does not tell us anything about the nature of the society that is organized. A State may be a little city like Lucca or a great Empire like Rome; a minute territory that has been formed out of the family possessions of some princely house, like Lichtenstein or Monaco, or a vast civilization like China, which has been for thousands of years a closed and self-sufficient world. We have only to look back over history and see the multiplicity and incommensurability of political organizations, to realize the absurdity of any international system which treats them all alike as though they were political individuals with equal rights and a common nature. To compare China with Liberia or the U.S.A. with the Dominican Republic, is like comparing the Bank of England with a village savings bank or an Atlantic liner with a fishing boat.

Now the comparison of such diverse forms may have a certain value for philosophical or scientific purposes, since it clarifies our ideas on the nature of boathood or bankness, but it is of no use for purposes of practical organization. If we attempted to organize the shipping industry on the principle of one vote per boat, we should merely disorganize the existing order and produce anarchy and chaos. And the same is true, though the absurdity is less flagrant, if we try to create an international organization based on the equal rights of nations, and as-

suming every *de facto* State to be a *de jure* nation.
Yet this is in effect what the League of Nations attempted to do, for we find among the original members of the League in the Treaty of Versailles, the
United States alongside Panama, Great Britain with
the Hedjaz, Italy and Liberia, France and Haiti.

If this was simply a concession to the temporary
needs of the post-war situation, it would not be so
important, but it goes much further than that, and
involves the basic sociological assumptions and ideals
of the modern international movement, whether in
its secular humanitarian or Catholic aspects. For
example, the clearest statement that I know of Catholic international principles—the Code of International Ethics prepared by the International Union
of Social Studies—while dealing exhaustively with
the rights and duties of States, gives superficial attention to the fundamental sociological problem of
the *nature* of the State. It accepts almost without
modification the Aristotelian conception of the city
State and applies it forthwith to the nation States
of modern Europe; so that the Augustinian *Domus,
Urbs, Orbis* is taken as an adequate classification of
the social structure of the modern world.

Now the Aristotelian political theory was based
on a fairly thorough analysis of the existing forms
of society, and even in the time of St. Augustine it
still retained its validity. Civilized society was still
organized on the basis of the city State, and the
Roman Empire formed a kind of world society composed of city States, which were the cells of the
international organism. Outside this was the chaotic

world of the barbarians who lived a kind of sub-political existence, and who were a continual threat to the civilized society of the Roman *orbis terrarum*. There remained one great civilized State—Persia, which was in a state of permanent hostility with Rome, and formed a sort of Oriental antithesis to the Roman world monarchy. This socio-political structure still retained its meaning for the medieval mind, in spite of the changes that had passed over the world. To medieval philosophers like St. Thomas, the city was still the essential political organ, and the place of the Roman Empire was taken by Christendom, which was regarded as the one universal society. Outside this there was Islam—the social Antichrist, with which the Christian world was in a state of permanent warfare, and there were the pagans of the East Baltic who were gradually conquered and incorporated, against their will, in the society of Christendom.

But at the close of the fifteenth century this traditional picture was suddenly shattered both within and without. Europe suddenly became conscious of a whole world of peoples, the savages of America and Africa, and the civilized peoples of the Far East, so that the scale of their historical and geographical universe was incalculably magnified. At the same time the Christian world was divided by heresy into warring camps, and out of the ruin of feudal principalities and free cities there arose the new monarchy armed with absolute power and endowed with the majesty of divine prerogative.

Henceforward the State—the typical political organism—was no longer the city, but the national monarchy. It had a distinctly imperial character and modelled itself rather on the pattern of the Roman Empire than of the city State. Nevertheless, it did not possess the universal character of the Empire, since its ambitions and claims were always limited by the existence of other similar States whose rights it acknowledged in theory, even though it might disregard them in practice.

Thus, though Christendom, in the medieval sense of a great Christian commonwealth ruled by a twofold hierarchy, no longer existed, its traditions were strong enough to form a cultural bond between the peoples of Europe which united them in a loose society of sovereign States. And in spite of all the changes that have passed over the world in the last two centuries with the rise of democracy and national self-consciousness, this social pattern still continues to mould our conception of political and international relations. Our idea of the State is still more or less derived from the Nation-States that were developed in Western Europe during the last four hundred years. Our ideas of international society and even of a World League of Nations, are still modelled on the pattern of the old European Society of States—while in the same way the new Nationalism of the non-European peoples is influenced both consciously and unconsciously by the example of European Nationalist States and their ideals.

Yet in reality these phenomena are profoundly different. India and China are not nations in the

same sense as Sweden or Ireland. They are cultural
unities that have no analogy *in* Europe except *with*
Europe itself. Turkey, on the other hand, has become a nation in the full Western sense, but it has
done so only by a complete breach with the past,
which has transformed the culture of the people no
less than the government of the State. And thus
Oriental Nationalism, which arose in protest and reaction against the European hegemony, is itself the
most striking proof of Europe's power to change the
world.

We must, however, face the fact that there is as
yet no world civilization in the same sense that there
has been a European civilization in the past. There
are powerful forces breaking down the old divisions
between peoples and cultures, but there are equally
powerful forces working in the opposite direction,
and these are threatening to disrupt and destroy the
unity of Western culture which has hitherto been the
real source of such international order as the world
has possessed.

3. European Unity and the League of Nations

We have seen that it is becoming increasingly difficult to apply the traditional political pattern of the
European past—a society of sovereign National States
sharing a common culture and a common spiritual
background—to a world of super States in which
rival races and civilizations struggle ruthlessly for
supremacy. The old European order may seem to be
irrational and disorderly, but it was held together
by a real respect for historic rights and precedents

and by the social prestige of monarchy which did much to counter-balance the inequality of political power between the greater and lesser States. But the revolutionary origin of the new form of State has destroyed the respect for historic right, while the opposition of principles and ideals leaves no common ground on which statesmen can meet as they could do in the court life of the old regime. The modern tendency for every State or group of States to identify itself with one of the rival types of political ideology is as fatal to any kind of world order as were the religious wars of the past. Indeed, it is even more fatal, since in the past the distinction between Church and State made it possible for States of different creeds to co-operate in matters of common political interest; whereas today the Totalitarian State is so closely identified with its ideology that it becomes impossible to distinguish between the warfare of ideas and the conflict of political interests.

If we accept the totalitarian principle, it would seem that the only hope of world peace is to be found in the triumph of a single ideology. And this was in fact the ideal of Communism in its earlier militant phase, when Zinoviev and Trotsky believed that the citadel of capitalism would fall at the first blast of the trumpets of the Red Army. But the last twenty years have proved the vanity of their hopes, and the actual result of the Communist offensive has been to accentuate the conflict of ideologies— to destroy or weaken the moderate parties and the constitutional States to the advantage of extremism and dictatorship.

Thus the attempt to unite the world by thrusting it into the strait-jacket of a uniform ideology is a utopian delusion which is reconcilable neither with international peace nor with national freedom. The true basis of international life is to be found not in ideological unity, but in community of culture. This was pointed out with remarkable clarity by Burke, when for the first time Europe was faced with a State that had consciously identified itself with a new political ideology. I will quote him at some length, as I am afraid one is obliged to take for granted that nobody reads Burke today, and the passage shows that the conception of Europe as a true community of culture is no novelty, but was treated as a fundamental truth by the classical Conservative thinkers of the past.

"Intercourse between nations," he writes, "does not depend so much as is generally supposed on the formality of treaties and compacts: nor is it merely a matter of political interest. Men are not tied to one another by paper and seals. They are led to associate by resemblances, by conformities, by sympathies. It is with nations as with individuals. Nothing is so strong a tie of amity between nation and nation as correspondence in laws, customs, manners and habits of life. They are obligations written in the heart. They approximate men to one another without their knowledge and sometimes against their intentions. The secret, unseen, but irrefragable bond of habitual intercourse holds them together even when

their perverse and litigious nature sets them to equivo-
cate, scuffle and fight about the terms of their written
obligations. With this similitude, peace is more of
peace and war is less of war. There have been periods
of time in which communities, apparently in peace
with each other, have been more perfectly separated
than, in later times, many nations of Europe have
been, in the course of long and bloody wars. The
cause must be sought in the similitude throughout
Europe of religion, laws and manners. At bottom
these are all the same. The writers on public law
have often called this aggregate of nations a commonwealth. They had reason. It is virtually one great
State having the same basis of general law; with
some diversity of provincial customs and local establishment."

And Burke then goes on to describe the different
elements of this community. First, the nations of
Europe have all had the same Christian religion.
Secondly, their polity and economy are derived from
the same sources, i.e., Germanic traditions embodied
in medieval institutions and finally ordered and clari-
fied by Roman law, so that in social constitution
the European States are far more alike than was generally realized. "From all these sources arose a system of manners and education that was nearly similar
in all this quarter of the globe, and which softened,
blended and harmonized the colour of the whole.

"From this resemblance in the modes of intercourse and in the whole form and fashion of life no
citizen of Europe could be altogether an exile in any

part of it . . . When a man travelled . . . from his own country he never felt himself quite abroad."*

Allowing for the oratorical and non-scientific form of Burke's treatment, I do not think that the essential problems of international relations have ever been more satisfactorily stated. The one point that vitiates Burke's treatment is the conservatism or traditionalism which led him, almost against his own principles, to regard the existing State system of the old regime as the only possible form of European order. He saw clearly enough the fallacies of revolutionary Liberalism, its neglect of historical reality, its utopian idealism, its false rationalism which caused it to attack Christianity and its one-sided individualism which made it ignore the organic character of social institutions.

But he failed to realize that the Revolution was not merely a negative revolt against Christendom and social order. It was also an assertion of the rights of the peoples against irresponsible government, and of the nations against the outworn traditions of the dynastic State.

And hence, when the Revolution had been defeated by the national forces that it had itself done so much to awaken, the allied statesmen at Vienna who were also Burke's pupils and disciples, also failed to take account of these forces. They recognized more fully than has ever been done before or since the existence of what Burke termed the European Commonwealth, but they organized Europe on the basis of precedent and dynastic legalism instead of as an

* *Letters on the Regicide Peace I* (ed. Payne III, pp. 80-81).

organic society of living nations. And consequently the growing force of the European national movements was left with no outlet, and their revolutionary explosions destroyed the artificial edifice of European order which the statesmen of Vienna had built up so carefully.

Now the League of Nations of 1919 repeated the error of the Holy Alliance by failing, in spite of its title, to recognize the existence of nations except in so far as they already possessed separate political existence. But in addition it ignored still more completely the existence of that European Commonwealth which the Holy Alliance had recognized and accepted as the basis of its international organization. This failure to recognize the vital importance of the historic culture-complex in international life left the League of Nations suspended in the air between the harsh realism of contemporary power politics and the cloudy idealism of cosmopolitan Liberalism. The result was that the League remained dependent in practice on an alliance of the victorious Powers, and that its decline has inevitably followed their loss of military and economic hegemony. Thus there has been a conflict between the ideals of the League and its real interests. League idealism favoured disarmament, a policy of international concessions and conciliation, and a tendency to treat every State as an equal partner in world fellowship. But in order to make the League system work under existing conditions, it was necessary to follow quite an opposite line of policy by aiming first and foremost at the preservation of the unchallengeable military supremacy of the group of Powers whose union was the only real foundation of the system.

In other words, the failure of the League was due to its real political-military basis being too narrow and one-sided and its ideal superstructure too universal and all-embracing. The essential task of the peacemakers of Versailles was to achieve a settlement on the basis of national self-determination which would, in however loose a form, restore the Commonwealth of Europe and provide the political conditions for economic and cultural co-operation. If this had been achieved, it would then have been possible to proceed further and to set up some kind of world organization "for the establishment of international law as the actual rule of conduct among governments" (to quote the words of the Covenant). It is possible that the United States, which refused to allow themselves to be entangled in European politics by the far-reaching commitments of the actual League, would have been ready to co-operate in a wider and more impartial organization of this kind, and would thus have made the creation of a real international order possible. For the failure of the League of Nations does not mean that the fundamental moral principle on which it was based can be abandoned. The principle which President Wilson invoked as the inspiration of his programme— "the principle of justice to all peoples and nationalities and their right to live on equal terms of liberty and safety with one another, whether they be strong or weak"—is a principle which nineteenth-century Liberalism inherited from the Christian tradition, and which has been once more proclaimed by Pius XII in his recent Encyclical as an essential principle of Christian civilization. It is this principle which we are defending today against the Totalitarian absolutism which, in the words of the Encyclical, "puts itself in the place of God and elevates the State or group into the last end of life, the supreme criterion of the moral and juridical order, and forbids every appeal to the principles of natural reason and of the Christian conscience."

The conflict which threatens to destroy civilization today is not a conflict of race or culture, or even ideology. It is a conflict of the naked will to power which has swallowed up all the ostensible ideological issues: the racial issue of Aryan *versus* Semite, the social issue of Communism *versus* Fascism, and the international issue between the supporters and opponents of the League of Nations. If this force is triumphant, it is the end of Europe, as a community of free peoples, for the saurian appetite of these monster Powers will inevitably swallow up all that is weak and destroy all that is strong. But also it is the end of any hope of international order in general, for the conflict that we are witnessing today is not merely a matter of European rivalries or interests. It is a world issue that is being fought out on European soil, but the effects of which cannot be limited to Europe.* The very idea of international law, as the modern world has known it, was the product of European civilization and has its ultimate

* This, of course, was written before the outbreak of war in the Pacific.

basis, like all the higher values of that civilization, in the belief in a transcendent spiritual order, in a natural and divine law to which States and peoples as well as individuals were subject.

As the Pope has said, it is only by a return to that law that the world can be saved from the abyss of disorder and destruction into which it is falling. And this is a much more fundamental problem than that of the League of Nations or any scheme of Federal Union. It is only when the moral principle of international law is accepted that we can go forward towards the creation of a system whether European or cosmopolitan, which embodies these principles in an institutional form. So that in the last resort, after the shipwreck of the existing pre-war ideologies, we come back to the ideological question on a deeper level—the assertion of the fundamental philosophical and moral principles on which not only Christian civilization but all civilization ultimately rests.

6

The Secularization of Western Culture

I<small>T IS</small> not possible to discuss the modern situation either from the point of view of religion or politics without using the word "culture." But the word has been used in so many different senses and is capable of so many shades of meaning that it is necessary to say something at the outset as to the sense in which I am going to use it, in order to avoid unnecessary confusion.

The Concise Oxford Dictionary gives three senses—tillage, improvement by mental or physical training, and intellectual development. None of these however is precisely the sense in which the word is used by anthropologists, sociologists, and now to an increasing extent also by historians and philosophers. From the date 1871, when Tyler in England published his famous book on Primitive Culture, and from a much earlier date on the Continent, the word has been extended to cover the whole complex of institutions and customs and beliefs, as well as arts and crafts and economic organization, which make up the social inheritance of a people. Thus it is almost interchangeable with the word civilization, except that the latter is as a rule restricted to the higher forms of culture, as there is an obvious objection to speaking of the "civilization" of an uncivilized people. I use Culture therefore as the wider and more inclusive term, and civilization as a particular type of culture in its higher and more conscious manifestations.

Thus it is possible to get behind or beyond civilization and study human nature in a relatively primitive state. But it is never possible to get beyond culture. The eighteenth century idea of a state of nature in which man existed before he got entangled in the meshes of the state and of organized religion, and into which he must think himself back in order to construct a rational order of society is of course completely mythical and unreal. Primitive man is just as much part of a social pattern, often a very elaborate one, and is just as much dependent on cultural traditions as civilized man, or even more so.

In the same way it is impossible to separate culture from religion, and the further we go back in history, or the lower we descend in the scale of social development, the more closely are they related to one another. It is easy to understand the reason for this which is inherent in the nature of religion itself. For religion is not, as the rationalists of the last two centuries believed, a secondary phenomenon which has arisen from the exploitation of human credulity, or as Hobbes put it "from opinion of Ghosts, Ignorance of second causes, Devotion towards what men fear and Taking of things Casuall for Prognostiques"; it lies at the very centre of human consciousness, in man's sense of his dependence on higher powers and of his relation to the spiritual world. The simpler a culture is the closer is its relation with religion, not of course because a low culture is more spiritual than the higher ones, but because the narrow limits of its control over nature increases man's sense of dependence, so that it seems impossible for society to exist without the help of the mysterious powers that surround him.

The relation between the higher and lower forms of religion has never been more perfectly stated than in the words of the Apostles to the simple Lycaonians, when they accepted Barnabas and Paul as Gods; "We preach that you should turn from these vanities to serve the living God who made heaven and earth and the sea and all things that are therein, who in times past suffered all nations to walk in their own ways. Nevertheless He left not Himself without witness in that He did good and gave us rains from heaven and fruitful seasons, filling our hearts with food and gladness." The religion of primitive man is concerned with just those things— food and rain and the course of the seasons. In them he sees the hand of God and the working of sacred and magical forces. Therefore the ways by which men live and the crises of their lives are inextricably interwoven with religious beliefs and practices to form the pattern of culture.

Nevertheless even the crudest and most primitive forms of religion are never completely restricted to this pattern; they always possess an element of transcendence without which they would cease to be religion. For since religion is the bond between man and God, between human society and the spiritual world, it always has a twofold aspect. To the outsider, whether he be a traveller or a rational critic, primitive religions seem like a dead weight of social convention and superstition which prevents the society from advancing; to the primitive himself, however, it is the way of the Gods, the traditional consecrated order which brings human life into communion with the higher powers; and we see from the history of more developed religions that the most simple and elementary religious practices are capable, not merely of becoming charged with religious emotion, but of becoming the vehicle of profound religious ideas, as for example the ritual of sacrifice in ancient India or the ceremonial ordering of the calendar in ancient China.

On the other hand, when we come to the higher religions where there is a conscious effort to assert the absolute transcendence of God and of the spiritual order, we still do not find any complete divorce between religion and culture. Even Buddhism, which seems at first sight to turn its back on human life and condemn all the natural values on which human culture is built, nevertheless has as great an influence on culture and impresses its character on the social life of the Tibetans or the Singhalese no less than a religion which adopts a frankly positive, or as we say "pagan" attitude towards nature and human life. Religions of this type do, however, bring out more clearly the element of tension and conflict in the relation between religion and culture, which it is easy to ignore in a primitive religion which seems completely fused and identified with the social pattern.

In neither type of culture therefore do we find anything that really corresponds to the problem that confronts us at the present day—the problem of a state of separation and dislocation between religion and culture; in other words the problem of a secularized culture. No doubt other cultures have passed through phases of relative secularization, e. g. China in the third century B.C., and Rome in the last age of the Republic. But these phases were confined to particular societies and almost certainly to small classes or elites in these societies. But today it is a world-wide phenomenon and, at least in the more advanced societies, it extends through the whole social structure and affects the life of the common people no less than the thought of the leading classes and groups.

Now it is easy enough to explain the universality of the present situation. It is due to the world-wide extension of Western civilization by imperial expansion, by material progress and by economic and intellectual penetration. But what is the relation between the immense extension of modern Western civilization and its secularization? Are they related as cause and effect? And if so is the extension the cause of the secularization, or vice versa?

There is no doubt that the rapid material progress and external expansion of Western culture has had a secularizing effect. World empires usually tend to lose touch with their spiritual roots, and the same is true of the expansion of a civilization by way of administrative and intellectual influence, as we see in the case of the Hellenistic world in the third and second centuries B.C. Nevertheless this is not the essential cause of the change. Western culture was becoming secularized before the great period of its expansion had begun. The fundamental causes of that process were spiritual and closely related to the whole spiritual development of Western Man. But the same causes which produced the secularization of culture were also responsible for its external expansion. They were, in fact, two aspects of a single process, a world revolution of such a tremendous kind that it seems to transcend history and create new categories with which our traditional standards of judgment are incapable of dealing.

It is with regard to the religious issue that the traditional methods of interpretation are most defective. For if we consider the problem from a Christian point of view we are faced by the paradox that it was a Christian culture and not a pagan one which was the source of this revolution. While the secular historian is brought up against the equally disturbing fact that the non-secular element in Western culture has been the dynamic element in the whole process of change, so that the complete secularization of culture by removing this element would bring the progressive movement to a full stop, and thus bring about a static society which has mastered social change to such a degree that it no longer possesses any vital momentum.

This is the greatness and misery of modern civilization—that it has conquered the world by losing its own soul, and that when its soul is lost it must lose the world as well. Western culture has never been a natural unity, like the great civilizations of the ancient east, like Egypt and China and India. It is a changing association of peoples and countries which owes its unity to the continuity of its tradition, a tradition which it did not even originate but which it inherited and transformed and enlarged until it became the source of a new world and a new humanity. For a thousand years the bearer of this tradition was the Christian Church, and during this formative period it was only by becoming members of the Church that the nations became partakers in the community of Western culture.

The importance of this factor has seldom been sufficiently appreciated by the historians. They recognized the influence of the Church on medieval history, and the way in which the religious unity of Christendom conditioned the development of the Western peoples. But, it seems to me, they have none of them fully realized the significance of the fact which is almost unique in world history, that Europe found its unity and cultural form not simply by the profession of a common faith, but by entering a spiritual community which was already existing and which possessed an independent principle of organization, with its own organs of authority and its own institutions and laws. The medieval Church was not a state within a state, but a super-political society of which the state was a subordinate, local, and limited organ. Ideally there was one great society—that of the Christian people—with a twofold hierarchy of spiritual and temporal ministers. And the spiritual conflict which occupied the medieval consciousness was concerned not merely with the relations of the two hierarchies to one another, but less consciously and more profoundly with the problem of reconciling this ideal order with the real world of territorial states and feudal principalities, which the descendants of the barbarians had built for themselves by the sword.

The existence of this double dualism—of Church and state and of Christian ideal and barbaric reality —is one of the main reasons why Western Christendom did not develop into a closed religious civilization like those of the ancient East. Instead, the unity of Christendom was broken and the cultural hegemony of the Church was destroyed by the religious revolution of the sixteenth century. But though this prepared the way for the secularization of culture, nothing could have been further from the mind and intention of the leaders of the movement. On the contrary, it seemed to them that they were working for the desecularization of the Church, and the restoration of Christianity to its primitive purity. They did not realize that the attempt to purify and separate religion from its cultural accretions, might find its counterpart in the separation of culture from religion and the increasing secularization of life and thought. And this was in fact what happened; though it was a gradual process which took centuries to complete itself.

Nevertheless the new lay humanist culture which was beginning to develop in the West in the fifteenth and sixteenth centuries was far from being entirely secular. As Burdach has shown the very conception of the Renaissance—or the rebirth of culture—was closely connected with the Reformation or the rebirth of Christianity. Both were influenced in their origins by the apocalyptic hopes of a spiritual renewal of Christendom, which was so widespread in the later Middle Ages and which found different forms of expression in Northern and Southern Europe. Neither the Humanists nor the Reformers dreamt of the destruction of Christendom. They believed, like Erasmus, that "the world was coming to its senses as if awakening out of a deep sleep," and they thought that religion and culture could slough off their old skins and could renew their youth by returning to their origins.

Thus the Renaissance achievement was like that of Columbus who discovered the new world by attempting to find his way back to the old world by a new route. The sudden removal of the fixed limits which had bounded the thought and action of medieval man, the opening of new worlds and the realization of the boundless possibilities of human reason caused a release of energies which gave Western culture a new world-embracing character. Though Western science was still in its infancy men like Leonardo da Vinci and Paracelsus and Campanella and Bacon had already begun to realize its world transforming possibilities.

Glory to Him who knows and can do all, writes Campanella:

O my art, grandchild to the primal Wisdom, give something of his fair image which is called Man.

A second God, the First's own miracle, he commands the depths; he mounts to Heaven without wings and counts its motions and measures and its natures.

The wind and the sea he has mastered and the earthly globe with pooped ship he encircles, conquers and beholds, barters and makes his prey.

He sets laws like a God. In his craft, he has given to silent parchment and to paper the power of speech and to distinguish time he gives tongue to brass.

The author of these verses is a striking example of the way in which the thought of the Renaissance united humanist and scientific culture with apocalyptic religious ideals and revolutionary hopes for a new order of society.

Throughout his long imprisonment of thirty years in the prisons of Spain and the Inquisition, Campanella continued to advocate his ideas of the coming of a new order which would unite mankind under the rule of nature. But even in its earliest and most revolutionary form Campanella's City of the Sun was far from being secular. It was a totalitarian communist theocracy governed by a priest king—the Metaphysician—elected by universal suffrage, and three magistrates representing the three divine hypostases—Power, Wisdom and Love—who deal respectively with war, science and education, and economics and eugenics. Neither property, marriage nor the family were admitted and the magistrates work according to aptitude, honours are given according to merit and food according to need and constitution.

At first sight the utopia of Campanella resembles that of Thomas More, but at the same time it differs profoundly in spirit and intention. It was not for the sake of utopia that Thomas More lost his head, but in defense of the traditional order of Christendom. But Campanella's utopianism had a definitely revolutionary character which showed itself in the fantastic attempt of a handful of friars and outlaws to overthrow the Spanish government in 1599, and to set up the City of the Sun on Mount Stilo in Catalonia. Thus I believe that Campanella more than Thomas More, and more than the Anabaptists of Muenster, should be regarded as the forerunner of modern revolutionary socialism, more especially as the idea of the organization and control of social life by natural science formed an essential part of his theory. Yet in spite of the revolutionary character of his thought, and in spite of its complete divorce from the cultural tradition of medieval Christendom, his ideal, as I have already said, was not a secular one. He looked back to the pagan identification of religion with culture, rather than forward to the modern secular state and the secularization of life. It was for this reason that he was so bitterly opposed to the Reformation, which he regarded as an individualist movement to desecularize religion inspired by the natural indiscipline of the Germanic people: in fact the new revolt of the barbarians.

For all his misunderstanding of the situation, there remains this element of truth: that in fact the chief cause of the secularization of Western culture was the loss of Christian unity—the dissolution of the community in which the peoples of the West had found their spiritual citizenship. The mere fact of this loss of unity created a neutral territory which gradually expanded till it came to include almost the whole of social life. The wars of religion and the long controversy concerning religious toleration, which produced such a prolific literature during the seventeenth century, especially in England, forced men to accept, at least as a practical necessity, the principle of common political and economic action by men who differed in their theological views and in their ecclesiastical allegiance; and when once men had admitted the principle that a heretic could be a good citizen (and even that an infidel could be a good man of business), they inevitably tended to regard this common ground of practical action as the real world, and the exclusive sphere of religion as a private world, whether of personal faith or merely private opinion.

In this way there arose the new liberal humanitarian culture which represents an intermediate stage between the religious unity of Christendom and a totally secularized world. On the continent it was at first the culture of the people; and in Catholic countries, at least, its permeation of society was accompanied by a violent revolutionary crisis. Only in England and North America did it proceed in the other direction—from below upwards—for there it found its inspiration not only in the rational idealism of the humanist tradition, but even more in the religious idealism of Puritanism with its conception of the Holy Community and of Christian Liberty.

But both these currents ultimately came together to form the liberal bourgeois culture of the nineteenth century, with its individualism and its Christian-humanitarian ethics, with its faith in reason and progress, in free trade and constitutional government. The place that religion held in this culture differed from country to country and from class to class. But on the whole I am inclined to think that there has been a tendency to underestimate its importance. In early Victorian England, for example, what struck the foreign observer was not simply the amount of religious observance, but the fact that Christianity influenced public policy. Thus a contemporary French statesman writes—"Religious convictions are not with them mere rules for private conduct or simply intellectual indulgences: they enter into political life and influence the actions of public men, as conscience weighs upon single individuals. The dissenting sects are generally the first to stir themselves energetically for some object, which in their eyes religion commands them to pursue. The movement even extends through the entire Christian Church of the country, then into the different classes of civil society, and finally reaches the Government itself, which either coincides from approbation or resigns itself to follow. Thus the traffic in slaves has been abolished; thus the spirit of peace has predominated in England until the last few years, gathering power at once from the wisdom of material interests and the force of religious convictions; and

imposed by the nation on the government, which on
its part, during the progress of this interval, has not
repulsed the public feeling but has voluntarily
adopted it as the rule of state policy."*

The fact that Liberal culture was founded on
Christian moral values rendered it accessible to religious influences, even in a secular age. Nevertheless
the spiritual elements in the Liberal culture were
not strong enough to control the immense forces
which had been released by the progress of the applied sciences and the new economic techniques. The
advent of the machine, which was in a sense the result of the liberal culture, proved fatal to the liberal
values and ideals, and ultimately to the social types
which had been the creators and bearers of the culture.

The machine involved the increase of power, the
concentration of power and the mechanization first of
economic life and then of social life in general. It is
true that in Britain and the United States the revolutionary effects of mechanization were reduced by the
existence of unlimited colonial territories and foreign
markets to absorb the new economic forces. It was
only when mechanization was applied in the closed
world of continental Europe that the revolutionary
character became plain. And this was above all the
case when it passed from the liberal bourgeoisie of
the West into the hands of the bureaucratic monarchies of Eastern Europe, which approached the

* Guizot, *Memoirs II*, 72. (English translation, 1859.)

problems of the new order from the standpoint of power politics and military organization.

The great conflict, that has divided Europe in the twentieth century and has produced two world wars, is the result of the application of similar technique in an opposite spirit and for opposite ends: science and mechanization being used, in the one case, in a commercial spirit for the increase of wealth; in the other, in a military spirit for the conquest of power. And as the conflict proceeds, the more complete becomes the mechanization of life, until total organization seems to be the necessary condition of social survival.

Liberal culture sought to avoid the danger of complete secularization by insisting on the preservation of a margin of individual freedom, which was immune from state control and to which, in theory at least, economic life was subordinated. And within the zone of individual freedom, religious freedom was the ultimate stronghold which defended the human personality. But the progress of mechanization and the social organization which it entails, has steadily reduced this margin of freedom, until today in the totalitarian states, and only to a slightly less degree in the democratic ones, social control extends to the whole of life and consciousness. And since this control is exercised in a utilitarian spirit for political, economic and military ends, the complete secularization of culture seems inevitable. That religion still survives is due on the one hand to the fact that the technique of social control is still not fully developed, so that there are holes and corners in society and in the human personality which have somehow escaped the process of regimentation, on the other hand, because religion itself is being used by the state as an instrument for social control, in much the same way as Augustus revived the moribund rites and institutions of Roman paganism in order to add the prestige of antiquity and tradition to his new order. But a religion of this kind which is being used either as a means to a political end, or at best as an instrument of culture, has lost its transcendent character and has thereby ceased to be a religion in the full sense.

Thus as I have suggested, the progress of Western civilization by science and power seems to lead to a state of total secularization, in which both religion and freedom simultaneously disappear. The discipline that the machine imposes on man is so strict that human nature itself is in danger of being mechanized and absorbed into the material process. Where this is accepted as an ineluctable historical necessity we get a society that is planned in a strictly scientific spirit, but it will be a static and lifeless order, which has no end beyond its own conservation and which must eventually cause the weakening of the human will and the sterilization of culture. On the other hand, if a society rejects this scientific determinism, and seeks to preserve and develop human vitality within the framework of a totalitarian state, it is forced, as in Nazi Germany, to exploit the irrational elements in society and human nature so that the forces of violence and aggressiveness, which all the cultures of the past sought to discipline and control, break loose to dominate and destroy the world.

This is the dilemma of a secularized culture, and we cannot avoid it either by a humanitarian idealism which shuts its eyes to the irrational side of life, or by a religion of personal spirituality which attempts to escape into a private world which is rapidly being liquidated and drained away by the social engineer.

Part II

THE RESTORATION OF A CHRISTIAN ORDER

1

Planning and Culture

THE conception of a planned society has had a revolutionary effect on social thought and political action during the last twenty years and its importance is still hardly realized by public opinion. Yet it is possible that it marks a change in human civilization greater than anything that has occurred since the end of the stone age and the rise of the archaic cultures of Egypt and Mesopotamia and the valleys of the Indus and the Yellow River.

No doubt it is implicit in the idea of applied science, as was already perceived by the men of the Renaissance such as Leonardo da Vinci, Campanella and Bacon. It is less evident in the following period owing to the eighteenth-century belief in a pre-established harmony between the natural and moral worlds which made individual interest an infallible guide to social good and regarded governmental action with suspicion. It was the nineteenth-century Socialists, above all the St. Simonians, who first popularized the idea and made it the basis of their social philosophy.

Finally it became a political reality in the twentieth century with the Russian Revolution and the rise of the totalitarian state. Above all the launching of the Five Year Plan by Stalin in 1928 aroused world-wide interest in the possibility of large-scale state planning and gave birth to a whole literature of propaganda and controversy on the subject.

The conception of social and economic planning was, however, by no means confined to Russia or to the Communists. It was accepted by the Western democracies as the solution of economic depression and unemployment and was the inspiration of President Roosevelt's New Deal in the United States; while in Germany it was applied with immense technical efficiency and ruthless force in order to remold the whole life of the nation according to Nazi ideas and to equip it for the task of world conquest and domination.

The revelation of the sinister possibilities of this scientific organization when it is exploited by totalitarian states has led to a certain reaction against the naïve idealization of planning as an infallible social panacea. There is a general recognition of the need to defend human freedom and spiritual values against the dehumanizing effects of a totalitarian organization of society. The original advocates of social planning in England and in America had been reformist socialists who still accepted liberal and humanitarian values and who did not look far beyond the elimination of the selfishness and confusion of the capitalist system. But when they saw it applied for very different ends of dictators and militarists, they were forced to revise their ideas. They began to realize that the liberal values that they had taken for granted were more closely related to the Christian values that they had discarded than they had believed, and that unless these values could be defended against the soul-destroying inhumanity of the new tyrannies all these achievements of scientific organization and social control would not only be worthless, but would be perverted into instruments of destruction and degradation. It is therefore time for us to reconsider the problem of planning in its wider implications.

The discussion has hitherto been mainly confined to the political and economic issues. The underlying problem of a planned culture has as yet hardly touched public opinion. And it is the instinctive recoil from a planned culture which is one of the strongest forces making against totalitarianism.

But one need not be a materialist in order to see that it is impossible to have a planned society without involving cultural as well as economic issues. You can limit your planning as the democratic states have done in the past, but then you also limit your economic planning. Any total economic planning means a planned society and therefore a planned culture. And it is this situation in which cultural planning is an extemporized affair that is forced on society by its planned economy without being willed or desired that is responsible for the crude and utilitarian character of modern culture.

For if we accept the principle of social planning from the bottom upwards without regard for spiritual values we are left with a machine-made culture which differs from one country to another only in so far as the process of mechanization is more or less perfected. To most people this is rather an appalling prospect, for the ordinary man does not regard the rationalization of life as the only good. On the contrary, men are often more attracted by the variety of life than by its rationality. Even if it were possible to solve all the material problems of life—poverty, unemployment and war—and to construct a uniform scientifically-organized world order, neither the strongest nor the highest elements in human nature would find satisfaction in it.

These views are usually dismissed by the progressive as reactionary. They are in fact the arguments of the conservative, the traditionalist and the romantic. They were first developed by Burke and the romantics against the social rationalism of Enlightenment and the French Revolution. But their criticism was based on a real sense of historical realities and they had, above all, a much clearer and deeper sense of the nature of culture than the philosophers whom they criticized.

They saw the immense richness and vitality of European culture in its manifold development in the different nations through the ages, and, in comparison, the philosophic ideal of a society founded on abstract rational principles seemed lifeless and empty.

And today even in spite of all the achievements of scientific technique and the increased possibilities of social control the problem still remains whether it is possible to produce by scientific planning a culture that will be as rich and varied and vital as one that has grown up unconsciously or half-consciously in the course of ages.

Comparing the modern planned society with the unplanned historical societies which it has succeeded we see that it is enormously superior in power and wealth, but it has two great weaknesses: (a) it seems to leave little or no room for personal freedom, and (b) it disregards spiritual values.

We see these twin defects most strongly marked in the totalitarian states, which have been absolutely ruthless in their treatment of personal rights. But wherever modern mechanized mass culture obtains, even in countries of liberal tradition, we find the freedom of the personality threatened by the pressure of economic forces, and the higher cultural values sacrificed to the lower standards of mass civilization. This is not simply a question of class conflict, for it is not only the life of the proletariat that is standardized. On the contrary, the most extreme forms of cultural standardization are to be found in the higher economic levels. The luxury hotel is the same all over the world and represents a thoroughly materialistic type of culture, while the inn which caters to the poorer classes has preserved its cultural individuality and national or local character to an exceptional degree.

The older type of culture was characterized by a great inequality in regard to individual freedom. Freedom was a manifold thing. There were all kinds of different freedoms. The noble, the bourgeois and the peasant each had his own freedom and his own constraints. On the whole there was a lot of freedom and no equality, while today there is a lot of equality and hardly any freedom.

Similarly the older type of culture had very little power over its environment, natural or social. But it had very clearly defined spiritual standards and was rich in cultural values. These were of course primarily religious, for religion was the supreme unifying force in the old type of society, but they were also cultural in the narrower sense, so that these societies had a much greater sense of style than our own.

Today we have made incalculable progress in the scientific control of our environment, but at the same time our culture has lost any clearly defined spiritual standards and aims, and our cultural values have become impoverished.

The old religiously orientated culture disintegrated two centuries and more ago, and now we see the same process of disintegration taking place with the liberal-humanist culture that was its successor and heir.

Nevertheless this disintegration of culture does not mean that modern social planning can ignore the cultural issue and content itself with economic and political reconstruction. On the contrary the fact that it has done so hitherto is one of the chief factors in cultural disintegration and this, in turn, is one of the main causes of disorder from which the modern world is suffering and which expresses itself in revolution and war.

A civilization which concentrates on means and neglects almost entirely to consider ends must inevitably become disintegrated and despiritualized.

Our democratic societies have done this, by devoting all their planning to the technical and industrial organization and leaving the sphere of culture to the private initiative of individuals, i.e. to unplanned activities. This was possible before the machine age, when the ruling class in society consisted of men of property in the old sense, men with a fixed economic background and a tradition of leisure, not unlike the citizen class of antiquity. But when this class had lost its economic foundation and was progressively absorbed into the machine order, it ceased to be culturally creative.

On the other hand the totalitarian states have instituted centralized planning for definite ends. But they have been even more crudely materialistic than the democratic states. Their plans are short-term plans, and consequently practical and utilitarian. In so far as they have undertaken cultural planning, they have subordinated it to these practical aims with the result that culture has been still further degraded and despiritualized. In the democracies there has undoubtedly been a loss and impoverishment of spiritual values. But in so far as they remain, they are free. We do not feel that religion and philosophy, art and science are being prostituted to serve the interests of a party or even of the state.

But it may be objected that this subordination of culture to statecraft is inseparable from the concept of planning. A free culture is an unplanned culture. The organization of culture means bringing it into the service of social ends and hence of the state.

This is the vital issue. Is it possible to develop a planned culture which will be free? Or does cultural planning necessarily involve a totalitarian state?

This is the question that Dr. Mannheim deals with in the final chapters of his book *Man and Society*. He points out that the origins of Totalitarianism are to be found in the military absolutism of the continent. "The army of the absolute states," he writes, "was the first great institution which not only devised rational methods for creating uniform mass behavior artificially by means of military discipline and other devices for overcoming fear, but also used these methods for educating large masses of men (who were taken for the most part from the lowest classes) to act and if possible to think in the way prescribed."*

This system of integrating a mass of individuals into a disciplined unity by compulsion is obviously the simplest and the most rudimentary, but peoples that have been trained in it are naturally more susceptible of totalitarian organization than the more democratic ones. So it is not surprising that the two great totalitarian societies of today are the revolutionary successors and heirs of the two greatest military monarchies of yesterday—i.e. Russia and Prussia. Whereas the two great democratic societies—the British Commonwealth and the U.S.A.—are essentially *civilian* states, which have never known (except in rare moments of emergency) the universal regimentation which is imposed by a militarist system.

But though this method of enforcing uniform organization by compulsory discipline is the easiest and gives the quickest results, it is not the most effective in the long run, not only because it leaves too little scope for individual adjustment, but because a society that is based on discipline and blind obedience has less internal resources and less power of moral resistance than a free society. If it is possible for a

* K. Mannheim, *Man and Society*, p. 255.

people to organize itself freely it will be stronger than one that is organized by force. It is the old story of the citizen soldiers of ancient Greece against the armies of Persia.

Now in the case of a modern planned society the problem is whether we can replace the enforced *Gleichschaltung* of the totalitarian dictatorships by a free co-ordination of all the social elements, a process which Dr. Mannheim compares to the orchestration of a symphony. But a symphony involves a composer as well as a conductor—and where is the composer to come from? It is, it seems to me, the ideal of the Philosopher King or the lawgiver of a Platonic Republic.

But who is there today who is able to act as the legislator of the spiritual world? Dr. Mannheim would agree that this problem is still unsolved and that the biologist and the economist are not capable of providing an answer. He looks rather to the rise of a new science of Social Psychology which will guide the legislator in the task not merely of organizing existing culture but also of transforming human nature to meet the new conditions of a planned order, since "it is only by remaking man himself that the reconstruction of society is possible." "At the present stage of events," he writes, "we need a new kind of foresight, a new technique for managing conflicts, together with a psychology, morality and plan of action in many ways completely different from those that have obtained in the past."

"While hitherto no particular group has had the responsibility of creating social integration—for anything that happened was the result of haphazard compromise between conflicting tendencies—today there are indications that if the groups engaged in politics still refuse to look beyond their own immediate interests, society will be doomed."*

It seems to me that Dr. Mannheim's solution raises two difficulties.

A. That a social science such as he desiderates hardly exists as yet, though we can see its beginnings.

B. That the remoulding of human nature is a task that far transcends politics, and that if the state is entrusted with this task it will inevitably destroy human freedom in a more fundamental way than even the totalitarian states have yet attempted to do.

Those states do, however, show us the risks of a wholesale planning which sacrifices the liberties and spiritual values of the older type of culture for the sake of power and immediate success. The planning of culture cannot be undertaken in a dictatorial spirit, like a rearmament plan. Since it is a much higher and more difficult task than any economic organization, it demands greater resources of powers of knowledge and understanding. It must, in fact, be undertaken in a really religious spirit.

Now it is clear that in the past in so far as culture was directed by conscious aims, it was above all religion that did it. In the Middle Ages religion did in fact create the cultural institutions that guided and controlled the mind of society, so that all the higher activities of culture were if not scientifically planned at least given spiritual form and unity.

* Op. cit. p. 15.

And in the Liberal-Humanist culture which formed the transitional stage between medieval Christendom and modern secular civilization, religion still retained great cultural importance. It was the source of the moral standards and spiritual values which are essential to the Liberal tradition, though Liberals frequently ignored this and attempted to base them on abstract ideas. But the rational ideals of Liberalism were abstracted from a historical religious tradition, and the Liberal culture was strongest and most enduring precisely in those societies in which the Christian social and political consciousness was most alive.

Nevertheless Liberalism prepared the way for the complete secularization of society by making a sharp division between the public world of economics and politics and the private world of religion and intellectual culture. It confined planning to the lower sphere and left the higher entirely free and entirely unorganized. Hence with the extension of planning and organization to the higher sphere, we are forced either to take account of religion in our schemes of social organization and therefore to desecularize culture; or to plan without any regard for religion and therefore to produce a totally secular culture, such as the Communists have evolved on the basis of economic Materialism.

Now in the days when the European social order was consciously religious, it preserved a dual social organization: It was recognized that the sphere of religion and of intellectual culture transcended the state. It had its own organization or spiritual society: the Church. This dual principle of organization had a far greater importance for European culture than is usually recognized. It was, no doubt, to some extent a source of conflict and tension. But it was a vital and healthy tension, which contributed in no small measure to the freedom of Western society and the richness of its culture.

It is obvious that modern culture is too secular, and modern religion is too divided for it to be possible to restore this principle directly by making the Church once again the all-embracing spiritual community that it once was. Any attempt to do this externally as a measure of social restoration would be an artificial construction, not a living spiritual principle. The territory that was formerly the domain of the Church, is now largely derelict. Religion has withdrawn into isolated strongholds, where it remains on the defensive, surveying the land through the narrow loopholes in the fortifications.

And the position of intellectual culture is no better. In a way it is worse, since its disintegration is more recent, and it has not had time to organize its defences as religion has done.

In fact at the present time it looks as though we were beginning to witness a sort of persecution of culture, corresponding to the anti-clerical and anti-religious movement of the last century. Of course the culture that is being attacked is by no means the same thing as the culture that we have been discussing. It is a sort of devitalized intellectualism which no longer possesses a social function or a sense of social responsibility.

A culture of this kind is a decadent and dying form

of culture, and it is bound to disappear. But that does not mean that society can exist without culture at all. It is all very well saying "To Hell with Culture," but that is just what has happened, and see where it has landed us! During the last thirty years the natural leaders of Western culture have been liquidated pretty thoroughly—on the battlefield, by firing squads, in concentration camps and in exile. A tough may be better than a highbrow, but a society that is dominated by toughs is not necessarily a tough society: it is more likely to be a disintegrated and disordered one. It is a phenomenon that is common enough in history, a typical phenomenon of periods of transition, and it is often followed by a sharp reaction which prepares the way for a spiritual renaissance.

Sooner or later, there must be a revival of culture and a reorganization of the spiritual life of Western society.

The more successful and complete is the process of economic organization the greater will be the need for a super-economic objective of social action. If man's increased control over his environment and his greater material resources are simply devoted to the quantitative multiplication of his material needs and satisfactions, civilization would end in a morass of collective self-indulgence. But the more natural and rational solution would be to devote the increased power and wealth and leisure that would emerge in a planned society towards cultural ends or, in other words, to the creation of a "good life" in the Aristotelian sense. For the higher culture is, after all, essentially the fruit of the surplus energy and resources of society. Cathedrals and theatres, universities and palaces—such things flower naturally from a healthy society as soon as it has acquired a bare margin of freedom and leisure.

It is obvious that the new planned society should be more and not less culturally creative than the societies of the past which accomplished such great things in spite of their poverty and weakness. The reason it has not been so hitherto has been due to our intense and one-sided preoccupation with the economic issue, which led to the starvation of all the non-economic functions and which also created the unemployment problem in the form in which we know it. But a planned culture which is the necessary complement to a planned economy would restore the balance of society since it would devote no less a degree of organized social effort and thought to the development of the non-economic functions. In this respect it would mark a return to the traditions of the pre-industrial age, which put a much higher social value on the non-economic functions than we have done in the West for the last century and more.

The question remains whether this task of cultural planning can be achieved, as Dr. Mannheim hopes, by a purely rational effort of scientific planning; or whether there is an element in culture and in human life which necessarily transcends planning, just as there are sub-rational and irrational ones which can only be planned mechanically.

In other words, will the culture of the future be

completely secularized, or will it be religious in a new way?

From the standpoint of the older rationalism, there is no question of super-rational elements. Religion is simply an expression of the irrational element in human nature—a dark and sinister power which is the enemy of true culture no less than of science.

Modern rationalism, however, adopts a somewhat different attitude. Today the emphasis is laid not so much on the irrationalism of religion, as on its sublimation of the irrational, but it is also criticized as escapism, wish-fulfillment—an illusory substitute for reality. If this were true, it would be useless to look to religion as a source of spiritual power; on the contrary, it would be a source of weakness, a kind of collective neurosis which perverts and saps social energy.*

But is it possible to reconcile such a view with the facts of history? For religion has undoubtedly been one of the greatest motive powers in human history. It seems to have increased collective energy rather than diminishing it, and whenever humanity has been on the move, religion has been like the pillar of fire and the cloud that went before the Israelites in their desert journeyings.

It seems to me impossible to believe that the power of the spirit is nothing but a perversion and consequently a degradation of physical energy, yet this is

* This is the Freudian view. Freud writes: "The religions of humanity must be classified as mass delusions of this kind," viz., delusional transformations of reality based on the desire to obtain assurance of happiness and protection from suffering. S. Freud, *Civilization, War and Death,* tr. J. Richman (1939), p. 34.

the logical conclusion of the rationalist argument. It is as though one were to say that reason itself arises from the perversion of the irrational. It is a line of thought that leads to the blank wall of nihilism and nonsense. Yet on the other hand if we admit the opposite principles—the creative powers of reason and the primacy of the spirit—we shall have to leave room in our planned world for the intervention of a power which transcends planning. And the only place for this power in a planned society is at the summit as the source of spiritual energy and the guiding principle of the whole development. For as economic planning is impossible unless a society possesses a certain amount of physical vitality—a will to live which provides the motive power for work, so cultural planning requires an analogous principle of spiritual life without which "culture" becomes a pale abstraction.

The only way to desecularize culture is by giving a spiritual aim to the whole system of organization, so that the machine becomes the servant of the spirit and not its enemy or its master. Obviously this is a tremendous task, but it is one that we cannot avoid facing in the near future. If culture is not to be dynamized from below by the exploitation of the subrational animal forces in human nature, it must be activized from above by being once more brought into relation with the forces of Divine power and wisdom and love. The faith in the possibility of this divine action on the world is the foundation of Christian thought. We believe that to every fresh need there is an answer of divine grace, and that every historical crisis (which is a crisis of human destiny!) is met by a new outpouring of the Spirit. The task of the Church and the task of the individual Christian is to prepare the way for such divine action, to open the windows of the human mind and remove the curtains of ignorance and selfishness which keep humanity asleep. The Gospels teach us how religion can act as the ally of human stupidity and ill will, how it can blind men's eyes and stop their ears. But we cannot use the Gospels as an argument for the failure of religion. On the contrary they prove that the power of the Spirit can break down any obstacles and overcome the most elaborate defenses that human ingenuity can devise. And while the present situation in many respects seems more difficult than any in past history, it is at the same time also more unstable, less fixed in custom and less emotionally attached. In fact the mechanization of human life renders it more sensitive to spiritual influence in some respects, than the old unorganized type of culture: at the present time this response is most evident where the forces in question are most evil, but clearly this cannot be the only possibility, and the great problem that we have to face is how to discover the means that are necessary to open this new world of apparently soulless and soul-destroying mechanism, to the spiritual world which stands so near to it.

2

Christian Social Principles

THE Christian Faith has always maintained the possibility of human salvation. Against the recurrent creeds of fatalism and materialism which have bound man's fate to the stars or to the earth, it has maintained man's freedom and his spiritual destiny. It has recognized more frankly than most human philosophies the reality of evil and the extent of the influence of evil on human nature. Nevertheless it has declared that this lustful carnivorous animal whose passions are infinitely more destructive and incalculable than those of the beasts of the jungle because they are guided by intelligence, is none the less *capax Dei*, capable of acquiring a spiritual nature and attaining a Divine end. Thus Christianity, more than any other religion, is characterized by its doctrine of spiritual renewal and regeneration. It stands for the restoration or transformation of human nature in Christ—in other words the creation of a new humanity.

This great central truth has been obscured and often forgotten by the religious individualism of the last two or three centuries, which conceived salvation as a happy after-life to be attained by pious individuals as the reward of their moral perfection, or their religious practices. But the Christian idea of salvation is essentially social. It has its roots in the Old Testament, in the conception of the People of God, and the prophetic teaching of the spiritual restoration of Israel, and the progressive manifestation of the divine purpose in history. It appears in the Gospel as the good news of the coming of the Kingdom—a Kingdom which was not national or political in the sense that the Jewish people conceived it, but universal and transcendent—a new spiritual order, destined to transform the world and humanity. And finally the theological and anthropological implications of this belief are fully developed in the Apostolic writings which declare the mystery of salvation, the mystery of the Incarnation, which is the birth of a new humanity and through which man is incorporated into the organic unity of the Divine Body.*

If this be the essence of the Christian doctrine of man's nature and destiny, it is clear that it must determine the Christian conception of history and social order. All temporal events and all the changes of culture are in some way to be related to this central reality. There is nothing human which is not affected by this divine revolution. *Emittes Spiritum Tuum et creabuntur et renovabis faciem terrae.*

The new world and the new humanity exist as a leaven or a seed under the surface of the present order—the order which Christians call the world. We believe that it is destined to transform it, that the time will come when the kingdoms of this world become the Kingdom of Christ and when all things will

---

* Cf. F. Prat, *La Théologie de St. Paul*, 2nd ed. 1912, I. p. 429 seqq. *Le Grand Mystère.*

be made new. The idea is no doubt hard to accept and even incredible from a purely human standpoint. Yet the world has experienced its truth once already. For what could have seemed more impossible than the transformation of the civilization of the ancient world by a group of obscure and uneducated men from a despised race in an obscure province? But none the less it happened; and after nineteen hundred years, after so many kingdoms and peoples have come and gone, it still in some degree affects our life and thought.

It will be said that this can't happen again. It happened once and it is done with: it has become a part of history. But this is not the Christian view. From that standpoint the conversion of the pagan world is only a specimen or a fore-taste of the world-transforming power of the Christian Faith and what is abnormal is the static and passive form of Christianity which the modern world takes for granted. But as we have seen, the modern world is the secularized world which has discarded Christianity as a part of the dead past and which has lost the sense of the spiritual values of the Christian tradition.

What we are facing today, however, is not the breakdown of the traditional culture of Christendom, it is the catastrophe of the secular culture which has taken its place. For the failure of our civilization to satisfy man's deeper needs has created a spiritual vacuum, a heat of darkness and chaos beneath the mechanical order and the scientific intelligence of the modern world. Hence the demand for a new order, for a total solution of our social problems, for a replanning of society which will transform human life and remake man himself. They are, in fact, symptoms of the fundamental religious need—the need of salvation—experiencing itself in new forms which correspond to the purely secular culture in which they have arisen. But if, as we have argued, the failure of modern civilization is directly related to its secularism and its loss of spiritual values, it is useless to set our hopes in remedies, however drastic, which ignore this fundamental problem. Therefore there is more occasion than ever before to assert the Christian alternative of spiritual renewal and spiritual order, for it is here and not in the region of political and economic organization that the real centre of the problem is to be found.

No doubt it is not easy for modern man to grasp the relevance of Christian principles to modern needs. The Church speaks a different language to that of the modern world, which has lost the very idea of theology. We must face the fact that the world of the Bible and the Fathers, and the dogmas of theology have become a dead language to the majority of men today. And this means that the great fundamental realities —the truths on which everything depends and which are more real than the things we see and touch—are dismissed as words, mere pious formulas that have no relevance to modern life.

Even from an external and superficial standpoint, it would be a mistake to allow a difficulty of this kind to prevent the comprehension of principles and ideas that have a real bearing on the fundamental issues of our time.

1. The Law of Nature

What are the main principles on which the Christian conception of social order is bound? In the first place there is the principle of the dependence of human life and human society on the Divine order: the idea of a Law of Nature by which all reasonable beings participate in the eternal Reason, the source and bond of the whole cosmic order.

This is a very old idea—so old that it has been treated as a universally accepted principle by lawyers and philosophers and theologians since the beginnings of our civilization. Nevertheless, it is challenged today in a very direct and radical fashion, and it may well be argued that this challenge is the fundamental moral issue of the present war. For the whole Nazi system with its exaltation of lawlessness and successful aggression, its assertion of the rights of the strong at the expense of the weak, and its cynical contempt for international law and treaties, is the denial of the traditional Western conception of Natural Law and is the expression of a diametrically opposite theory.

According to this view law is a political act which merely expresses the will of the community or the state. The state's will is law, and since the state wills its own self-preservation and its own advantage, the law is not based on "justice" but on the will to power and the will to live. And so we get another "law of nature," a law which is non-moral because it is the expression of the same irrational life force which makes the wild beasts devour one another and insects thrive on the suffering and destruction of higher organisms.

Everything therefore depends on whether we believe in the existence of a spiritual order of which man is naturally conscious by his knowledge of good and evil, or whether the world runs blind, driven by irrational forces which man must serve if he is to survive.

According to the first alternative it is clear that states and nations no less than individuals are bound by a higher law than self-interest and self-preservation. There is an eternal law that governs all things and is, as it were, the reason of the universe. In this order man participates consciously in so far as he is a rational and moral being, and it is the source from which all human laws derive their ultimate sanction. As St. Augustine says in a famous passage in "The City of God," "Since God from Whom is all being, form and order has left neither Heaven nor Earth, nor angel nor man, nor the lowest of creatures, neither the bird's feather, nor the flower of the grass nor the leaf of the tree without its due harmony of parts, and without, as it were, a certain peace, it cannot be believed that He should have willed the Kingdoms of men and their government and subjection to be outside the laws of His providence."

It is true that St. Augustine recognized only too clearly that man's history is a black record, and that even the relative peace and order that had been conferred on the ancient world by the Roman Empire had been purchased only by a vast expenditure of blood and human suffering. The empire was, in fact, not the creation of justice, but of the will to power. Nevertheless, in so far as it was not satisfied with power alone, but aspired to rule by law, it recognized the principle of justice which implies the existence of moral principles and of the eternal laws on which they are based.

This is the meaning of Natural Law in the traditional Catholic sense. It is a very simple doctrine since it merely asserts—to use the words of St. Thomas— that "there is in men a certain natural law, which is a participation of the eternal law by which men discern good and evil." Without this power of moral discernment man would not be a reasonable being. But this does not mean that it provides a ready-made code of rules which everyone everywhere admits. The moral sense varies according to the measure of the understanding, and differences of education and culture and character affect the one no less than the other. Hence St. Thomas admits that the Natural Law may be obscured or perverted by social causes; as an example he quotes Caesar on the Germans who did not "regard robbery as unjust so long as it was carried on outside the frontiers of the State, but rather as a laudable form of youth activity."* But although man's moral consciousness is limited and conditioned by social factors it is never entirely extinguished; just as man remains a rational being even in a state of barbarism which seems to the civilized man to be little higher than that of an animal. And as every man by his reason has some knowledge of truth, so every man by nature has some knowledge of good and evil, which

* Caesar *De Bello Gallico*, VI. 25.

makes it possible for him to adhere to or deviate from the universal order.

As I said at the beginning, this idea of Natural Law is so fundamental that it was accepted as a self-evident truth by theologians and lawyers alike from the period of the Roman Empire down to modern times. Thus Cicero bases his whole theory of law on the doctrine that human law is nothing but the application of a law which is founded on nature and on the eternal law of God, and which is no more affected by the will of the rulers, the decisions of judges, the will of the people, than is the course of nature. In the same way, 1800 years later Blackstone, the embodiment of English legal traditionalism and commonsense, declares that the "law of nature being coeval with mankind and dictated by God Himself is, of course, superior in obligation to any other. It is binding all over the globe in all countries and at all times; no human laws are of any validity, if contrary to this."*

How did the sacred and secular tradition come to be abandoned—as for the most part it has been abandoned—by the modern world? Its enemies come from very different camps, yet their agreement on this issue is something more than an accident and corresponds to a very deep cleavage in European thought. On the one hand, it had its origin in one element of Protestant and specifically Lutheran thought, i.e. the doctrine of the total depravity of human nature and the dualism, or, rather, contradiction of Nature and Grace which leaves the former a helpless prey to the powers of evil, until it is rescued by the violent ir-

* Introduction to the *Commentaries*.

ruption of divine grace. The effect of this dualism is
to divorce the moral law from religion, so that it possesses a purely temporal value. As Luther puts it,
the law belongs to the earth, the Gospel belongs to
heaven, and they are to be kept as far separate as possible. "In civil government we must most rigidly
exact and observe obedience to the law, and in that
department we must know nothing either of gospel
or conscience or grace or forgiveness of sins, or even
of Christ himself; but we must know only how to
speak of Moses, the law and works. Thus both things,
to wit, the Law and the Gospel are to be severed as
far as possible one from the other and each is to remain in the separate place to which it appertains. The
Law is to remain out of heaven, that is to say, out of
the heart and the conscience; on the other hand, the
freedom of the Gospel is to remain out of the world,
that is to say, out of the body and its members."*

The profound pessimism of Luther saw in Nature
nothing but the kingdom of death and the Law of
Nature as a law of wrath and punishment, and thus
his extreme supernaturalism prepared the way for the
secularization of the world and the abolition of objective standards.

But the revolt against Natural Law did not only
spring from the otherworldliness of Luther and the
Reformers. It found an even more powerful support
in the worldliness of the Renaissance statesmen and
thinkers. Already before the Reformation Machiavelli had produced his Intelligent Man's Guide to
Politics which studies the art of government as a non-

* *Commentary on Galatians.*

moral technique for the acquisition and maintenance of power, thus depriving the state of its religious character as the temporal organ of divine justice and making the interests of the state the supreme law by which all political acts must be judged. This is the source of the "new jurisprudence" which took the place of the common law of Christendom and which, as Leo XIII explained in his political encyclicals* undermined the moral foundations of Western civilization.

It leaves no room for the consecration of the state to God which is so solemnly and sacramentally expressed by the traditional rite of the coronation of Christian kings. On the contrary, it involved the secularization of the state and the desecration of law and authority. By emancipating the prince from subordination to a higher order, it destroyed both the principle of order and the principle of freedom in the state itself.

This false political realism which denies or ignores spiritual realities is no less fatal to the Christian tradition and no less destructive of Christendom as a social reality than was the false spiritualism of Luther. Indeed, its influence has been wider and deeper, since it has not been restricted to certain countries and peoples, but has influenced the thought of Catholics and Protestants alike, and has grown stronger with the progressive secularizing of our civilization. The thought of Luther belongs to a different world from that in which we live; he was still a man of the Middle Ages, though he was in revolt against medieval

* e.g. *Immortale Dei,* and *Libertas Praestantissimum.*

Catholicism. But the thought of Machiavelli is still alive in the modern world and finds expression in the words and deeds of modern politicians and dictators. As Pius XII writes in his Encyclical "Darkness over the Earth," "Today the false views held in earlier times have been amalgamated with new invention and misconception of the human mind. And this perverse process has been pushed so far that nothing is left but confusion and disorder. One leading mistake we may single out as the fountain head, deeply hidden, from which the evils of the modern State derive their origin. Both in private life and in the State itself and, moreover, in the mutual relations of State with State and country with country, the one universal standard of morality is set aside, by which we mean the Natural Law, now buried away under a mass of destructive criticism and neglect."

2. *The Idea of Christendom*

I have already pointed out the historical causes of this revolt against the classical Catholic conception of Natural Law and their intimate relation with the breakdown of the religious unity of medieval Christendom in the sixteenth century. Today we are witnessing a resurgence of this revolutionary criticism of Natural Law, both in the religious and the secular spheres so that it has become one of the most sharply contested points of Catholic doctrine. In so far as this criticism is Christian, e.g. in the case of Karl Barth and his British disciples, it is partly due to a misconception of the place of the doctrine in Catholic theory.

It has never been regarded as a complete and all-embracing basis of Christian social theory. It is essentially partial and limited. When the Church comes to consider the problems of Christian social life and the ideal of a Christian culture, she considers civilization not as a static order based on the unchanging precepts of Natural Law, but as a concrete historical reality which derives its moral values and even its spiritual unity from its religious tradition.

In spite of the amount of study that has been devoted in recent years to the social doctrine of the Papal Encyclicals, comparatively little attention has been given to this side of their teaching on Christian civilization. Nevertheless it runs through the whole series of Encyclicals from 1878 to the present day and it is impossible to understand their teaching on international order without it. It is based on the idea that Europe is essentially a society of Christian peoples or nations—a society which derives its unity not from race or economic interest but from spiritual community, and that it is only by a restoration of this spiritual foundation that European order can be restored.

In the words of Benedict XV, "It is the teaching of history that when the Church pervaded with her spirit the ancient and barbarous nations of Europe, little by little the many and varied differences that divided them were diminished and their quarrels extinguished; in time they formed a homogeneous society from which sprang Christian Europe which, under the guidance and auspices of the Church, whilst preserving a diversity of nations, tended to a unity that favoured its prosperity and glory."*

Thus though Christian civilization is not the end of Christianity, it is in point of fact the fruit of Christianity. For, as Pius X wrote in 1905,** there are many benefits in the natural order that without being the direct object of the Church's mission nevertheless flow from it as its natural consequences. For "the Church, while preaching Jesus crucified, who was a stumbling-block and folly to the world, has been the first inspirer and promoter of civilization. She has spread it wherever her apostles have preached, preserving and perfecting what was good in ancient pagan civilization, rescuing from barbarism and raising to a form of civilized society the new peoples who took refuge in her maternal bosom, and giving to the whole of human society, little by little no doubt, but with a sure and ever onward march, that characteristic stamp which it still everywhere preserves. The civilization of the world is Christian civilization; the more frankly Christian it is, so much is it more true, more lasting and more productive of precious fruit; the more it withdraws from the Christian ideal, so much the feebler is it, to the great detriment of society.

"Thus by the intrinsic force of things, the Church becomes again in fact the guardian and protector of Christian civilization. This truth was recognized and

* *Pacem Dei Munus Pulcherrimum,* May 23, 1920, in "The Pope and the People," p. 228.
** *Il Fermo Proposito,* June 11, 1905. "The Pope and the People," pp. 190-191.

admitted in former times; it even formed the immovable foundation of civil legislation. On it rested the relations of Church and States, the public recognition of the authority of the Church in all matters relating in any way to conscience, the subordination of all State laws to the divine laws of the Gospel, the harmony of the two powers, civil and ecclesiastical, for procuring the temporal well-being of the nations without injury to their eternal welfare."*

This conception of a Christian civilization which is not an abstract ideal but a real historical tradition, embodied in social institutions and manifesting itself in a many-sided cultural activity, is the idea of Christendom. Whether we accept it or reject it as an ideal, we cannot deny its historical reality, as the great source of European unity—the pit from which we were digged and the rock from which we were hewn. Even Gibbon, whom nobody will accuse of undue sympathy for the Christian element in our civilization, bears witness to this and shows how religion and the authority of the Popes, "cemented the union of the Christian Republic; and gradually produced the similar manners and common jurisprudence which have distinguished from the rest of mankind the independent and even hostile nations of modern Europe."

But though Europe derives its form, its spiritual unity and its culture from the Christian tradition, it is no longer Christendom: or rather it is Christendom in a state of disintegration and dissolution. For according to the Encyclicals European culture

* *Il Fermo Proposito,* June 11, 1905.

cannot remain itself when it is deprived of its religious foundation. Christianity is the soul of Western civilization, and when the soul is gone the body putrefies. What is at stake is not the external profession of Christianity, but the inner bond which holds society together, which links man to man and the order of the state to the order of nature. And when this has gone nothing remains but the principle of brute force which is essentially unreconcilable with a pluralist society like the European community and which therefore operates as a revolutionary and destructive force alike in the social and the international order: dividing class against class and nation against nation, until either society is destroyed or humanity is reduced to a dead level of servitude under the iron hand of power. For more than sixty years successive Popes have warned the modern world of the approaching catastrophe* and now the catastrophe has come.

The optimism which filled the nineteenth century with its dreams of a humanitarian utopia of material progress and rational enlightenment no longer deceives anybody. On the contrary, there is a danger that we should fall into the opposite extremes of defeatism and despair. It is therefore important not to lose sight of the positive side of the Papal teaching, to remember that the Holy See has never despaired of the Christian republic but, as Leo XIII said "has set itself as a wall and a bulwark to save human society from falling back into barbarism."

For if European civilization derives its life and

*e.g. Leo XIII First Encyclical *Inscrutabili,* 1878.

unity from a higher spiritual principle, it is not bound to the fatal cycle of birth and death, it has in a sense an immortal soul—at least a possibility of spiritual renewal. "To restore all things in Christ," wrote Pius X in the Encyclical that I have already quoted, "has always been the Church's motto, and it is especially ours in the dangerous times in which we live . . . to restore in Christ not only what directly depends on the divine mission of the Church to lead souls to God but also as we have explained, that which flows naturally from this divine mission, i.e. Christian civilization, in each and all of the elements that compose it."

Thus the apparent apostasy of Christendom and the social and political catastrophes that have followed do not destroy the possibility of restoration. They may even prepare the way for it by bringing down the walls and towers that man has constructed as the refuges of his selfishness and the fortresses of his pride. Amongst the wreckage the foundations of a Christian order still remain; for it is based on the eternal Law of Nature which is the law of God and the changeless needs of human nature. We have on our side, said the Pope in his broadcast appeal on the eve of war, not only the spirit of old Europe which has preserved the faith and genius of Christianity, but the whole human race which hungers for bread and liberty not for steel. On the other side the principles which have undermined and destroyed the Christian order are, as the Pope shows in his Encylical "Darkness over the Earth," not merely negative but actually unnatural. For both the denial of the

Brotherhood of Man and the assertion of the omnipotence and absolutism of the State have their origin
in the denial of the Natural Law which, as Leo XIII
teaches, is the source and standard alike of human
law and human liberty.* What made Christian Europe a true society of nations was its recognition of
this supreme law which transcended national differences and the interests of governments. For though
as Benedict XV says the law was often violated in
practice, though there were wars and revolutions and
acts of social injustice without number, nevertheless
the sanctity of law was acknowledged by the conscience of Christendom so that it provided an objective standard by which the nations were judged.**

Without justice the state is nothing but organized
robbery and the law of nations nothing but the law
of the destruction of the weak. Today the rights of
nations are ignored because Europe no longer possesses a common moral standard. It is true that a
real effort was made after the last war to restore international order on the basis of justice to all peoples
and nationalities and their right to live on equal
terms of liberty and safety with one another whether
they be strong or weak—principles which are entirely in conformity with those of the Encyclicals.
But the League of Nations failed to restore a Christian order because it ignored the spiritual aspect of
the problem; it created a juridical skeleton of international order, but not the living body of a spiritual

* On Liberty.
** *Ubi Arcano Dei.* The Pope and the People, p. 244, cf. Pius XII
Darkness over the Earth.

community. As the present Pope has said "Even the best and most detailed regulations will be imperfect and foredoomed to failure unless the peoples and those who govern them submit willingly to the influence of that Spirit which alone can give life, authority and binding force to the dead letter of agreements."* And the result was that the League failed to overcome the drift to anarchy and war and revolution and in its place there arose the monstrous development of totalitarian absolutism which, in the Pope's words, votes itself into the privileges of Omnipotence and "treats the state or the general body of citizens as the end to which all human action must tend and the rule by which all moral and legal questions must be judged."** If this development is triumphant it is the end of Christendom, the end of Europe as a community of free peoples, the end of civilization itself. Its defeat depends in the last resort, not on the force of arms but on the power of the Spirit, the mysterious influence which alone can change human nature and renew the face of the earth.

3. The Power of the Spirit

For, from the Christian point of view, the failure of the League of Nations and the frustration of all the other attempts made by men of good will to create a just social and international order are an inevitable result of the progressive secularization of modern culture. As Pius XII has pointed out in his

* *The Pope's Five Peace Points*, p. 15. (C.T.S.)
** *Darkness over the Earth*, p. 22.

Encyclical "Darkness over the Earth," the effects of this process cannot be limited to the theological sphere. The loss of faith in God is followed by the loss of universal moral principles and finally by the loss of all that binds man to man. For lack of faith in God, the nations fall asunder and destroy each other. They try to be gods themselves, when they are but leviathans—sub-human monsters whose immense strength is guided by no spiritual power.

> It will come
> Humanity must prey upon itself
> Like Monsters of the deep.

Our civilization is falling into the power of these blind forces because it has lost the Spirit which is the source of life and light. As the Pope has said, no political arrangements, no new order, no league of nations, no international institution will help us unless we realize this and submit to this power which alone can give life, authority, and binding force to the dead letter of the law. But how can this be done? Is it possible for a world which is so old and disillusioned and unfaithful to renew its youth and be born again in the spirit? It is the question of Nicodemus: "How can such things be?" And the answer is the same for peoples and civilizations as for individuals. "The Spirit breatheth where he will and thou hearest his voice, but thou knowest not whence he cometh or whither he goeth." We cannot set limits to God's power or deny the possibility of His creative action. Nor, on the other hand, can we decide beforehand how we shall act in relation to the new tasks which we as a nation or a group may be called upon to undertake.

In the Old Testament the prophets were continually warning the Jews against trusting in the efficiency of political action and against relying on "the arm of the flesh" or expecting "the day of man," yet on the other hand they condemned no less strongly the faint-hearted and mean-spirited refusal to ask great things of God and to expect His salvation in the face of overwhelming difficulties and disasters.

Today we are faced by a new situation which demands new methods of action. We have to arm ourselves for a spiritual conflict with the organized forces of evil, which as St. Paul says are not merely material or human, but are themselves spiritual, "world rulers of darkness," whose subtle and violent attack overwhelms the fragile barriers of a human order and civilization which has denied their very existence.

To those who see in evil nothing but an abstract generalization of the faults and weaknesses of individuals, it is natural that the Christian solution should also seem vague and obscure. But if we recognize the tremendous reality of the evils that we have to face, we shall see that the power of the Spirit is the only power that can overcome them.

We are passing through one of the great turning points of history—a judgment of the nations as terrible as any of those which the prophets described. We see all the resources of science and technology of which we were so proud devoted methodically to the destruction of our world. And behind this material destruction there are even greater evils, the loss of freedom and the loss of hope, the enslavement of whole peoples to an inhuman order of violence and oppression. Yet however dark the prospect appears we know that the ultimate decision does not rest with man but with God and that it is not His will to leave humanity to its own destructive impulses or to the slavery of the powers of evil. God not only rules history, He intervenes as an actor in history and the mystery of the Divine Redemption is the key to His creative action. For the Kingship of Christ and His authority over the nations are not pious phrases: they are principles of revolutionary importance for the political as well as the moral order. As Newman wrote a hundred years ago: "Christ's religion was not a mere creed or philosophy. A creed or a philosophy need not have interfered with kingdoms of this world; but might have existed under the Roman Empire or under the Persian. No; Christ's kingdom was a counter kingdom. It occupied ground; it claimed to rule over those whom hitherto this world's governments ruled over without rival: and if this world's governments would not themselves acknowledge and submit to its rule, and rule under and according to its laws, it 'broke in pieces' these governments—not by carnal weapons but by Divine power."

3

The Sword of the Spirit

WE HAVE seen that the Christian view of man and society is far from being a static traditionalism, as its rationalist critics have so often supposed. What distinguishes the Christian view of history from that of secular philosophy is above all the belief in the divine government of the world and the intervention of the Spirit in history and in the power of man to resist or co-operate with this divine action. These conceptions are most clearly expressed in the prophets of Israel, who are in a special sense the bearers of the Sword of the Spirit. For the Prophets not only give an interpretation of history in terms of the Kingdom of God and the divine judgment, they also show the power of God manifesting itself above all in the prophetic Word.

The Voice said Cry. And he said, What shall I cry?
All flesh is grass, and all the glory of it like the grass of
the field.
The grass withereth, the flower fadeth because the Spirit
of the Lord bloweth upon it.
Surely the people is grass.
The grass withereth, the flower fadeth, but the Word of
the Lord shall stand for ever.

In all the crises that changed the course of history

they saw the hand of God, and for each crisis there was also a corresponding Word which it was the mission of the prophets to declare. If God withheld His Word, or if it was perverted by false prophets, the course of history ran blind.

The prophet that hath a dream, let him tell a dream, and he that hath my word, let him speak my word faithfully. What hath the chaff to do with the wheat, saith the Lord?

Is not my word like a fire, saith the Lord, and like a hammer that breaks the rocks in pieces?

But the Word of God was not only the word of judgment and destruction, it was also a creative force, the Word of Life, the organ of the spirit which renews the face of the world, as we see in Ezechiel's vision of the valley of bones: the dry bones of the House of Israel, when the holy city had been destroyed and the people were exiles and captives who had lost their hope.

And He said to me: Prophesy to the spirit, prophesy, O son of man and say to the spirit: Thus saith the Lord God: Come Spirit from the four winds and breathe upon these slain that they may live.

Here we have a really dynamic vitalism, in comparison with which the new biological vitalism of blood and race and the old pagan vitalism of the gods of the earth are weak and degraded and obscure. The Spirit blows through the world like wind and fire, driving the kingdoms before it, burning up the works of man like dry grass, but the meaning of history is found not in the wind or in the fire. but in "the small voice" of the Word which is never silent, but which cannot bear fruit unless man co-operates by an act of faith and spiritual obedience. This dynamic and prophetic element is an essential part of the Christian tradition, and it is present even in periods when the Church seemed bound to a fixed and changeless social order, as in Eastern Christendom. But today it has acquired fresh importance owing to the breaking down of the partition which divided the religious and secular spheres of life during recent centuries and the coming together of the inner world of spiritual experience and the outer world of historic events in a new unity.

Today Christianity is implicated in history just as much as Israel was in the age of the prophets, though there has not yet been time for Christians to adjust their minds to what has happened. Nevertheless, there is already a general realization that social and political issues have become spiritual issues —that the Church cannot abstain from intervention without betraying its mission. The reason for this great change is not, however, primarily religious— that is to say, it is not due to the advance of the Christian element in our culture and the reconquest of the world for God. Quite the contrary. It is due to the invasion of the spiritual by the temporal, the triumphant self-assertion of secular civilization and of the secular state against spiritual values and against the Church. The real meaning of what we call totalitarianism and the totalitarian state is the total control of all human activities and all human energies, spiritual as well as physical, by the State, and their direction to whatever ends are dictated by its interests, or rather the interests of the ruling party or clique.

Such an attempt has been made by the despots of the past—for the God-state is the oldest of all the enemies of God. But in the past the power of the state was limited by the means at its disposal. Today it is unlimited. For the advance of science and technology, while it has immeasurably increased man's control of his environment, has also increased the control of society over the individual, of the State over society, and of the rulers over the State. In the new States not only a man's property and his work, but his family, his leisure and his thought are controlled by the immense and complex machinery of party and police and propaganda which are gradually transforming society from a commonwealth of free citizens into a hive or an ant-heap. For the new tyranny is not merely a matter of subjugating the people by force to the rule of a master, like the tyrannies of the past; it uses the new techniques of psychology and behaviourism to condition the personality and to control the mind, as it were, from within. By continued repression and stimulation, by suggestion and terrorization, the personality is subjected to a methodical psychological assault until it surrenders its freedom and becomes a puppet which shouts and marches and hates and dies at its masters' voice, or in response to their unseen and unrecognized stimulation. In such an order there can be no place for religion unless religion forfeits its spiritual freedom and allows itself to be used by the new power as a means for conditioning and controlling the psychic life of the masses. But this is an impossible solution for the Christian, since it would be a sin against the Holy Ghost in the most absolute sense. Therefore the Church must once more take up her prophetic office and bear witness to the Word even if it means the judgment of the nations and an open war with the powers of the world.

The Western democracies and their leaders gravely underestimated the revolutionary force that drove the totalitarian states forward with the result that the old European states system has collapsed like a house of cards and we are fighting for our existence against a ruthless enemy. And, similarly, Christians have failed to realize how profoundly the moral foundations of the world had been shaken and what a tremendous effort was needed in order to save humanity from the abyss of nihilism and spiritual disintegration. These two struggles are indeed not the same. For it is possible that the defeat of Germany might leave the spiritual evils of totalitarianism as strong as ever, while war is itself a destructive element which favours the progress of the spirit of nihilism and destruction. Everything depends on whether it is possible to use the temporal struggle, not for destructive or purely material ends, but as a means of checking the demonic forces that have been let loose on the world. For, as Burke wrote a century and a half ago, no material gain is sufficient to outweigh the cost of war, which is the lives of men. "The blood of man should never be shed but to redeem the blood of man. It is well shed for our family, for our friends, for our God, for our country, for our kind. The rest is vanity; the rest is crime." If this is true of the limited wars of the past, it is much more so of total war with its monstrous burden of destruction. This immense evil is only bearable if it is the only means of preventing or ending still greater evils. And this, in fact, is what we believe, for I think it is difficult to deny that the majority of Englishmen, whatever their religious beliefs, feel that they are defending not only their lives and property, but things that are greater than themselves; and deeper than political or economic interests. They believe that they are standing against violence and treachery and injustice in the cause of all mankind.

If the ordinary man is prepared to stake everything, as he has done, for this obscurely felt, but real, faith, the Christian is bound in faith and honour to do no less in the spiritual conflict that lies behind the battle of the nations and to bear witness to the Word of God at whatever cost. This is the fundamental aim of the Movement of the Sword of the Spirit, which has taken as its title the words of St. Paul, where he speaks of the spiritual armament for the war that is fought "not against flesh and blood but against principalities and powers, against the rulers of the world of this darkness, against spiritual wickedness in high places." As Cardinal Hinsley said in the address which inaugurated the movement:

The Apostle wrote these words in prison chained between two Roman soldiers in their warlike array. He says in effect that the gross panoply of warfare or material armaments count for little against the Spirit, for the word of God is not bound down, *Verbum Dei non est alligatum.* The spirit cannot be enslaved or imprisoned except by its own wilful betrayal. The Sword of the Spirit is the Word of God, and the Word of God is more piercing than a two-edged sword.

If Christians had realized this truth and had made it their principle of action, the evils that now threaten to overwhelm us would never have arisen. But this is just the truth which the modern world has denied. It has put its trust in the "arm of flesh" like the Jews of the Old Testament, it has believed the word of man rather than the Word of God. It has reversed the whole hierarchy of spiritual values so that our civilization has been turned backwards and upside down, with its face towards darkness and nonentity and its back to the sun of truth and the source of being. For a short time—whether we reckon it in decades or centuries is of small importance—it remained precariously skating on the thin ice of rationalism and secular humanism. Now the ice has broken and we are being carried down the flood, though we may delude ourselves that the forces that have been released are of our own creation and serve our will to power.

Is it possible to reverse this process? No human power can stop this progress to the abyss. It can only come about by a profound movement of change or conversion which brings the human spirit once more into vital relation with the spirit of God.

Every world crisis, is, as the word denotes, a judgment and a decision out of which something new

must come. It is therefore an opportunity to hear
the Word of God and for the Spirit to manifest its
creative power to humanity. This is the hope that
the prophets always maintain in their vision of
judgment against the nations, and which the Church
constantly repeats in the liturgy. "Come, O Lord,
do not wait, deliver thy people from the hand of
power. Show thy face and we shall be saved." This
tremendous sense of urgent need and real deliverance
finds only a very pallid and vague reflection in the
religious attitude of the average Christian. That is
why the Christian faith has made so little impression
on the modern world and seems powerless to influence the course of history. And although the
Movement of the Sword of the Spirit may seem in
itself a very small thing, I think it is important, because it does attempt to face this vital issue which
has been so neglected and ignored by the more
highly organized forms of ecclesiastical activity. As
Cardinal Hinsley says, everyone can play a part in
this spiritual crusade, for the Spirit divides His gifts
to each according to his will to use them. We can
take part in it by prayer, by study and by action.
It is not necessary to say much about the first and
last of these, for all Catholics understand the importance of prayer, and all Englishmen understand
the importance of action. But both Catholics and
Englishmen are inclined to neglect the second intellectual arm and to undervalue the importance of
the power of thought. The real reason of the success
of the new powers that are conquering the world
and the failure of Christians to withstand them has

been that the former have used the intellectual arm to the fullest extent, however perverted their aim, whereas the Christians have been content with good intentions and sound principles which they have accepted as a matter of course. It was the greatest of the dictators, Napoleon, who said: "There are two powers in the world, the sword and the mind. In the long run the sword is always beaten by the mind." Yet no one can accuse Napoleon of undervaluing the power of the sword. And so the fact that we believe the power of the Spirit is even greater than that of the mind is no reason for neglecting the latter, which can be either the most potent instrument of the Spirit or its most formidable adversary.

The attempt of the mind to dispense with the Spirit, to build a world that should be entirely in man's power and should find its end in him, is no new thing. It is, as St. Augustine showed, a universal tendency that runs through the whole of history and takes on different forms in different ages. But never has it revealed itself so explicitly as it does today in the totalitarian state, which has almost succeeded in constructing a world completely closed to the Spirit and leaving no loophole or corner for spiritual freedom. But the result is so oppressive to human nature, so ultimately self-destructive, that it must inevitably produce a reaction of resistance and revolt, in which the Christian elements in Western civilization will once more make themselves felt. It may seem utopian at this time to speak of the coming of a new Christian order—a new Christendom. But the more we recognize our distance from the goal and the immensity of the difficulties to be overcome, the more hope there is of ultimate success.

For what we must look for is not the alliance of the temporal power, as in the old Christendom, and an external conformity to Christian standards, but a re-ordering of all the elements of human life and civilization by the power of the Spirit: the birth of a true community which is neither an inorganic mass of individuals nor a mechanized organization of power, but a living spiritual order.

The ideal of such a community was the dream that inspired the political reformers and revolutionaries of the last two centuries, but since they rejected the power of the Spirit their ideals proved unreal and utopian, and they achieved either freedom without order, or order without freedom.

Today, we are fighting against the totalitarian order, which is the most radical and systematic denial of freedom that the world has seen. But we must recognize while we fight for freedom that freedom alone will not save the world. A true peace can only be secured by the restoration of spiritual order, for it is only in the Spirit that power and freedom are reconciled and united, so that the Sword of the Spirit is both the power that can deliver us from the hand of the enemy and the force that awakens and sets free the dormant sources of energy in human nature itself.

4

Return to Christian Unity

I F THE Christian faith contains such vast sources of spiritual energy and power, if the Church is the divine organ of world transformation and the seed of a new humanity, how has it come about that the world—above all the Christian world—has fallen into its present plight? From the Christian point of view it is easy to understand persecution and external adversity and failure, but it is far harder to face the failure of Christianity on the spiritual plane. For it is not simply that modern civilization has become secularized, it is that Christians have allowed civilization to become secular. In the past the Church provided the spiritual leaders and teachers of Europe. It controlled the universities, it possessed in every town and village in every land of Christendom a centre of instruction for the preaching of the Gospel and the formation of Christian opinion. If this has been lost, as it has been lost, almost entirely, we cannot refuse all responsibility and put the blame on the shoulders of the rationalists and the anticlericals. For as I have pointed out in Chapter III, the primary cause of the secularization of Western culture has been the religious divisions between Christians. Behind the present crisis in the life of Europe there lie centuries of religious disunity and strife which have divided men's minds in the spiritual order itself and which have destroyed the bond of charity which alone can transcend the conflict of material interests and the corporate selfishness of classes and peoples.

The return to Christianity is therefore the indispensable condition for the restoration of a spiritual order and for the realization of the spiritual community which should be a source of new life for our civilization.

This principle is accepted in theory by all sincere Christians, but in practice there are profound differences of opinion, not only between Catholics and Protestants, but even among Catholics and among Protestants, both as to the methods by which unity can be achieved and as to the extent to which Christians can co-operate in spite of their divisions in common action to meet the present crisis of civilization.

There is a heavy responsibility on Christians to make their voice heard in this hour of darkness. Otherwise the word will pass to the hard and hateful voice of God's adversary who is also called "the accuser of the brethren." The divisions of Christians have always given him plenty of grounds of accusation and if we allow these divisions to silence or confuse our witness, we are surrendering and betraying our cause at the decisive point and moment.

Nevertheless the fact remains that Christians differ in matters of belief and in matters of order. They are divided by centuries upon centuries of strife and controversy. There has been persecution and counter-persecution. Rivers of blood have flowed and all these ancient errors and divisions and enmities have left their traces like the scars of old wounds and mutilations on the body of Christendom. Such a situation evokes two contrary attitudes to the problem of Christian co-operation. On the one hand, there are those who are in revolt against Christendom's black record of dissension and strife and who believe that the primary condition of common action is for Christians to renounce their differences and unite at once on the basis of the truths they hold in common which in their view form the essence of Christianity. On the other hand, there are those to whom the divisions between Christians are real and so important that they obscure the existence of any common element. Christianity is nothing but a name —which is used to cover a number of different religions which have not necessarily got more in common with one another than with other religions which are not termed Christian.

Clearly neither of these extreme positions is acceptable to us and they both fail in the same way, viz. by underestimating the importance of religious belief. The undenominationalist view tends to what the Catholic theologians call "indifferentism"—that religious beliefs don't matter and that the will to co-operate is everything. The rigorist view concentrates its attention so much on the question of authority and ecclesiastical order that it ignores or undervalues the importance of the common beliefs, the common moral values, the common religious traditions and the common sacraments and forms of worship that exist in the midst of the religious divisions of the Christian world. We have the clear apostolic testimony as to the fundamental criterion of Christianity: "By this the Spirit of God is known. Every spirit that confesses that Jesus Christ has come in the flesh is of God; and every spirit which denies Jesus is not of God and this is Antichrist."

Today we have to face Antichrist in a new form—the totalitarian Antichrist or the total organization of human society on anti-Christian principles. This is the enemy which the Sword of the Spirit exists to combat and therefore it should be the common cause of all who confess the name of Christ. Here without any compromise of principles or any narrow exclusiveness there is a clear case of co-operation on the deepest and most spiritual grounds.

"They are of the world: Therefore of the world they speak and the world heareth them." "You are of God and have overcome him. Because greater is He that is in you than he that is in the world."

Nevertheless the appeal of the Sword of the Spirit is not confined to the Christians to whom it is primarily addressed. For the new Antichrist is also the enemy of God and man and every man who is in any degree conscious of a higher law than that of force and national or individual interest has the right and duty to join in this crusade. This is the Natural Law basis, which has been referred to so often, and which is expounded at length in the Papal Encyclicals. I will here quote only the passage from Pius XI's Encyclical on the Church in Germany since it is most directly relevant to the question that we are dealing with.

"It is a trend of the present day to dissociate more and more, not only moral teaching, but also the foundations of law and justice from the true faith in God and from the revealed commandments of God. Here we have in mind especially what is usually called Natural Law, written by the finger of the Creator Himself on the tables of man's heart (Rom. 2.14 etc.) which sound human reason not blinded by sins and passions can read on these tables. By the commandments of this natural law every positive law, whoever may be the lawgiver, can be tested as to its moral content and consequently as to the lawfulness of its authority and as to its obligation in conscience. Those human laws which are irreconcilably opposed to natural law have an innate defect which can be cured neither by compulsion nor by any external display of force. By this standard we must judge also the fundamental principle: 'Right is what is advantageous to the people.' It is true a right meaning may be given to this principle if it is understood to mean that what is morally illicit can never be to the true advantage of the people. Even ancient paganism recognized that the maxim to be perfectly accurate should be inverted and should read: 'Nothing is ever advantageous if at the same time it is not morally good, but because it is morally good it is also useful' (Cicero, *De Officiis* III.30). This fundamental principle, cut off from moral law, would mean in relations between states a perpetual state of war amongst the various nations; in the life of the state it confuses advantage and right, and refuses to recognize the fundamental fact that man as a person possesses rights given him by God which must be preserved from every attempt by the community to deny, suppress, or hinder their exercise. To overlook this truth is to lose sight of the fact that the true common good is ultimately defined and discovered from the nature of man with its harmonious co-ordination of personal rights and social obligations, as well as from the purpose of society which is determined by the same human nature. Society is willed by the Creator as a means to the full development of the faculties of the individual, and a man has to make use of society, now giving and again taking for his own good and for the good of others. Nay more, those higher and more universal values which cannot be realized by individuals but only by society are intended by the Creator ultimately for the sake of the ultimate end of man, for his natural and supernatural development and perfection. Whoever transgresses this order shakes the pillars of society and imperils its tranquillity, security, and even its existence.

"The believer has an inalienable right to profess his faith and to practise it in the manner suited to him. Laws which suppress or render difficult the profession and practice of this faith are contrary to natural law." (*Mit brennender Sorge* 34 and 35).

It will be noticed that this passage concludes with a strong affirmation of the right of religious freedom. This question has proved one of the stumbling blocks in the way of Christian co-operation in the Sword of the Spirit since it has been felt that Catholics have failed to recognize this principle. It is however clear from this passage and from the whole doctrine of the Sword of the Spirit that on this particular issue there is no difference of opinion between Catholic and Protestant, and each is equally concerned to defend spiritual freedom against what Pius XI calls "the thousand forms of organized religious bondage," "the lack of truthful news and of the normal means of defence," (*ibid.* 8) which are characteristic of the totalitarian state. No doubt there is a great difference of opinion between Catholics and Free Churchmen as regards the rights and privileges which an established Church can justly claim. But the same difference exists in a slightly different form between the Free Churches and the Church of England, or the established Lutheran churches on the Continent. But these differences are no reason for refusing to combine against a danger that threatens alike the religious freedom of the great historic Churches of Christendom with their tradition of power and privilege and the rights of the humblest and smallest religious bodies which have suffered persecution again and again in the course of their history.

It is clear to me that religious freedom is one of those "principles of human liberty and the Natural Law" which are laid down in the Constitution as the fundamental aims of the movement, and if that be admitted, it is surely a waste of time or worse to dispute with one another about causes of friction which are political rather than religious in origin. We must, however, remember that the principles of Natural

Law, essential as they are, are only the minimal basis of common action. The real appeal of the Sword of the Spirit is to the grace and power of God which alone are strong enough to oppose and to defeat those powers of spiritual darkness of which St. Paul writes in the passage from the Epistle to the Ephesians from which the Sword of the Spirit has derived its name. No secular remedy can meet the world's need; no purely moral effort can restore true peace and spiritual order to society. The only final end to which Christian action can be directed is the restoration of all things in Christ. All Catholic teaching on social action during the present century has been based on the doctrine of the universal Kingship of Christ, which is the Church's answer to the universal claims of the totalitarian systems. But in spite of its tremendous implications this doctrine should not be an obstacle to Christian co-operation: it is a principle of unity, not of division, for in so far as the Kingship of Christ is recognized not as a theological abstraction but as a social reality, the divisions of Christendom will be transcended and the human race will realize its organic unity under its Divine Head.

Now this goal of spiritual unity may seem infintely remote from the facts of the real world, the reality of a civilization that has turned away from God and has become the servant of demonic forces. It seems infinitely remote even from the facts of the religious world which is so grievously divided and disintegrated. Nevertheless this vision of unity is not merely a kind of Christian Utopianism; it is a living spiritual reality which can no more be denied or destroyed than the unity of the human race in the natural order. As a Catholic theologian has recently written: *"All* men are at heart potentially members of Christ, therefore of His Body the Church. And that potentiality is not merely a remote purely abstract possibility. The activating principle, the Power of Christ and His Spirit is everywhere present. So too is the freedom to accept or reject. The universal Motherhood is open to all, but it rejects none."*

We believe that the creation of this divine society is of infinitely greater importance than anything else in known history and that it is only in this society that mankind can be delivered from the curse of misunderstanding and fratricidal strife which has been the lot of fallen humanity. And the spirit of this society which is charity is the only power which is capable of giving new life, "by this we know that we have passed from death to life, because we love the brethren."

Now the present world crisis must be judged by Christians in relation to these fundamental truths. We must ourselves take our share of the responsibility. We have failed to make our voices heard before the nations. We have allowed "the blessed vision of peace, the City of God whose king is Truth, whose law is Charity, whose frontier is Eternity," to be hidden behind the dust of controversy and narrowed to the field of our own feeble and partial sight.

* "Membership of the Church." Victor White, O. P., Blackfriars, Sept. 1941. p. 468.

Yet however unfaithful Christians may have been in the past and in the present to their mission, we believe that the transforming and regenerating power of the Spirit is still present in Christ's Church, and that if we do our part God will once more manifest this power in answer to the world's great need.

2

But it may be objected that the collaboration of Christians on this basis of fundamental principles is impossible, because it ignores the real nature of our disagreement. Granted that Catholics, Anglicans, Orthodox, Lutherans and Free Churchmen all believe in the Church of the Living God as the pillar and ground of the truth, the fact remains that it is not the same Church in an objective institutional sense that is the object of this faith. We see this most clearly in the case of Catholics and Orthodox. Here are two perfectly concrete and definite organized spiritual societies which agree to a remarkable extent in their conception of their nature and office, but which are mutually exclusive, so that it would seem that the more profound is their belief in "the Church," the more complete is their separation from one another. In the case of the Protestant denominations and especially the Free Churches, the situation is of course far less clearly defined, owing to the complete disappearance of structural and intellectual unity. Nevertheless it is conceivable that reaction against the fissiparous tendency of Protestantism, of which reaction the Œcumenical Movement is the most striking example, might result in the creation of a reunited Protestant Christendom, which would stand over against the Catholic Church, in the same way that Eastern Orthodoxy has done in the past.

Thus we are brought up once more against the fundamental problem of Christian disunity which is the problem of schism. In practice this problem is so closely associated with that of heresy, i.e. difference of religious belief, that they are apt to be confused with one another. But it is nevertheless important to distinguish them carefully, and to consider the nature of schism in itself, for I believe that it is in the question of schism rather than that of heresy that the key to the problem of the disunity of Christendom is to be found. For heresy as a rule is not the cause of schism but an excuse for it, or rather a rationalization of it. Behind every heresy lies some kind of social conflict, and it is only by the resolution of this conflict that unity can be restored.

In order to illustrate what I mean I would take as an example the schism between the Byzantine and the Armenian churches, for that controversy is sufficiently remote for us to treat it in a completely impartial spirit. Here the theological issues at stake were the Monophysite heresy and the decrees of the council of Chalcedon; matters of the highest importance which involved the most profound and subtle problems of theological science. Yet even from the beginning it is obvious that the passions which filled the streets of Alexandria with tumult and bloodshed and set bishops fighting like wild animals were not inspired by a pure desire for theological truth or even by purely religious motives of any kind. It was a spirit of faction which used theological slogans, but which drew its real force from the same kind of motive which causes political strife or even war and revolution.

And when we leave the primary conflict at Alexandria and Ephesus and come to its secondary results in Armenia or Abyssinia, it is obvious that the theological element has become practically negligible, and the real conflict is one of national feeling. Take as an example the rubric, which used to appear in the Greek liturgy for the week before Septuagesima Sunday and which I quoted in *The Making of Europe*: "On this day the thrice accursed Armenians begin their blasphemous fast which they call artziburion, but we eat cheese and eggs in order to refute their heresy." Here, it seems to me, we can see in an almost pure state the spirit which causes religious dissension. To put it crudely, it means that the Greeks thought the Armenians beastly people, who were sure to be wrong whatever they did. And where such a spirit reigns what could be hoped for from theological discussions? The same spirit which made the eating of cheese a confutation of Armenian depravity would never have any difficulty in finding some theological expression, and if it had not been the doctrine of the Incarnation, then something else would have served just as well.

Now it is easy for us to condemn the Greeks and the Armenians, because we belong to a different world, and if we fast at all, we find it difficult to understand how people can attach such enormous importance to the questions of exactly when and how the fast is made. But can we be sure that the same spirit is not just as strong today, though it takes quite different forms? I remember, years ago, reading a story of an eminent Nonconformist divine whose name I have forgotten, which struck me as an example of this. He had been on a visit to Assisi and was immensely impressed with the story of St. Francis and the medieval art in which it is expressed. But one evening, as he was visiting the lower church, he happened to come across a friar and a group of peasant women making the Stations of the Cross and singing one of those mournful traditional chants which are so different from our English hymn tunes, and strike one as half Oriental. And suddenly he experienced a violent revulsion of feeling and said to himself: "This religion is not my religion and this God is not the God that I worship."

This seems to me a perfect instance of what I have in mind because the intellectual or theological motive is entirely absent. It is not as though he jibbed at Mariolatry or the pomp of a High Mass. He was revolted by the very thing in Italy for which Evangelical Nonconformity has stood in England, a spontaneous manifestation of popular Christocentric devotion. And what upset him was not any divergence of theological views but merely the alien setting and the different cultural tradition which separates the world of the Italian peasant from that of the well-to-do middle-class Englishman.

There is no need to labour the point. It was realized only too forcibly by the writers and thinkers of the Enlightenment from Bayle to Gibbon and

Thomas Paine, and it was largely responsible for the reaction against orthodoxy in the eighteenth century. But, unfortunately, its use as a weapon against revealed religion has tended to blind orthodox apologetics to its real significance. History has shown that no true solution is to be found in the direction which the eighteenth-century Enlightenment took, i.e., by constructing a purely rational philosophy of religion based on the abstract generalities that are common to all forms of religion. For deism is nothing but the ghost of religion which haunts the grave of dead faith and lost hope. Any real religion must recognize, on the one hand, the objective character of religious truth—and hence the necessity of a theology—and on the other, the need for religion to embody itself in concrete forms appropriate to the national character and the cultural tradition of the people. It is right that Italian peasants and the English shopkeepers should express their feelings in different forms; what is wrong is that they should worship different gods or should regard each other as separated from the mind of Christ and the body of the Church because they speak a different language and respond to different emotional stimuli. In other words: difference of rite ought not to involve differences of faith.

Now it is hardly necessary to point out the bearing that this has on the problem of the reunion of Catholic and Protestant Europe. To the average Protestant Catholicism is not the religion of St. Thomas and St. Francis de Sales and Bossuet; it is the religion of Wops and Dagoes who worship the images of the Madonna and do whatever their priests tell them to.

And the same is true of the average Catholic, *mutatis mutandis*.

Underlying the theological issues that divide Catholicism and Protestantism there is the great cultural schism between Northern and Southern Europe which would still have existed if Christianity never had existed, but which, when it exists, inevitably translates itself into religious terms.

Yet this division is a natural one which cannot be condemned as necessarily evil since it is part of the historical process. If it had been possible to keep life to a dead level of uniformity, in which Englishmen and Spaniards, Frenchmen and Germans, were all alike, conditions might be more favourable to religious unity, but European civilization would have been immensely poorer and less vital, and its religious life would probably have been impoverished and devitalized as well. It is the besetting sin of the idealist to sacrifice reality to his ideals; to reject life because it fails to come up to his ideal; and this vice is just as prevalent among religious idealists as secular ones. If we condemn the principle of diversity or polarity in history, and demand an abstract uniform civilization which will obviate the risk of wars and religious schisms, we are offending against life in the same way as though we condemned the difference of the sexes, as many heretics actually have done, because it leads to immorality. And this is not a bad parallel, because the polarity or duality of culture of which I have spoken is but an example of that universal rhythm of life which finds its most striking expression in the division of the sexes. Of course

I do not mean to say that the duality of culture is an absolute, fixed, unalterable law; it is rather a tendency which acts differently in different societies and in different stages of the development of a single society. But this is a tendency which is always present and which seems to become more clearly defined when social life and culture is most vital and creative, as, for example, at the time of the Renaissance.

Any vital point in the life of society may become the centre of such a polarization, and where a culture has an exceptionally rigid organization, as in the Byzantine empire, the principle of duality may find expression in an apparently arbitrary division, like those of the Circus factions—the Blues and the Greens—which played so important a part in the social life of Constantinople. As a rule, however, race and religion are the vital points around which the opposing forces in society coalesce. Thus we see how the Ionian and Dorian strains form the two opposite poles of Greek civilization and finally become defined in the conflict between Athens and Sparta which tore Greece asunder in the fifth century B.C.

Sometimes the two types of motive coalesce and reinforce one another, as in Ireland, where the cause of religion and race became identified, so that the opposition between Celt and Anglo-Saxon finds religious expression in the opposition of Catholic and Protestant. We find a similar state of things in Poland, where it was twofold, and showed itself in the conflict of Catholic Pole and Orthodox Russian in the East, while in the South, where the conflict was a purely national one between Catholic Pole and Catholic Austrian, feeling was less intense and the cultural opposition less strongly marked. On the other hand in Bohemia at an earlier period, where the opposition of Czech and German also manifested itself in a religious form, Slav nationalism took an heretical form and the German ascendancy was identified with the cause of the Church.

But, in addition to these cases, where the principle of social polarity is exemplified in its crudest form, we have a more subtle kind of socio-religious polarity which develops inside the unified national society and within the boundaries of a common religious tradition. A most striking example of this is to be found in England, where the tension of opposing social forces found expression in the religious opposition between the Established and the Nonconformist Churches. At first sight it may seem as though the diversity and disunity of Nonconformity are inconsistent with what I have said about religious schism as an expression of duality of culture and the tendency of social forces to converge round two opposite poles. But if we leave aside the theological aspect of Nonconformity and concentrate our attention on its social character we shall see that the opposition of Church and Chapel, of conformity and dissent, has an importance in the life of the eighteenth- and nineteenth-century English village or small town which far outweighs the differences between the various Nonconformist sects. And to some extent at least this religious opposition forms a spiritual background or foundation for the political division between the great English parties, so that in many parts of England it was taken for granted that a Nonconformist would be a good Liberal and a Churchman would be a good Conservative. It is true that this does not hold good of the early period of Methodism, but Methodism arose at a time when the Whigs represented the established social order, and it owes its importance to the fact that it made its chief appeal to the disenfranchised classes to whom the political parties of the day made no direct appeal.

But, whatever view we may take of the causes of any particular schism and the social significance of particular religious movements, there can, I think, be no question but that in the history of Christendom from the Patristic period down to modern times, heresy and schism have derived their main impulse from sociological causes, so that a statesman who found a way to satisfy the national aspirations of the Czechs in the fifteenth century, or those of the Egyptians in the fifth, would have done more to reduce the centrifugal force of the Hussite or the Monophysite movements than a theologian who made the most brilliant and convincing defence of Communion in One Kind or of the doctrine of the two natures of Christ. Whereas it is very doubtful if the converse is true, for even if the Egyptians had accepted the doctrine of Chalcedon they would have found some other ground of division so long as the sociological motive for division remained unaltered.

What bearing has all this on the problem of Reunion as it exists today? It would be a profound mistake to conclude that because religious disunion in the past has been based on social and political

causes, we must accept it in a spirit of fatalism, as
an evil which cannot be remedied except by political
or economic means. The cause of Christian unity
can best be served neither by religious controversy
nor by political action, but by the theological virtues: faith, hope and charity. And these virtues must
be applied both in the intellectual and the religious
spheres. It is, above all, necessary to free the religious
issue of all the extraneous motives that take their
rise in unconscious social conflicts, for if we can
do this we shall deprive the spirit of schism of its
dynamic force. If we can understand the reason of
our instinctive antipathy to other religious bodies,
we shall find that the purely religious and theological obstacles to reunion become less formidable and
more easy to remove. But so long as the unconscious
element of social conflict remains unresolved, religion is at the mercy of the blind forces of hatred
and suspicion which may assume really pathological
forms. If it seems that this is an exaggeration you
have only to look back at our own past and consider
the history of the Gordon Riots or the Popish Plot.

Hence the first and greatest step towards religious
unity is an internal and spiritual one: the purging
of the mind from the lower motives which may con-
taminate our faith. For in the vast majority of cases
the sin of schism does not arise from a conscious
intention to separate oneself from the true Church,
but from allowing the mind to become so occupied
and clouded by instinctive enmities or oppositions
that we can no longer see spiritual issues clearly, and

our religious attitude becomes determined by forces that are not religious at all.

It is easy enough to see, in the fifteenth century, for example, how vested interests and material motives caused the leaders both of Church and State to oppose necessary reforms, but it is no less evident that the passion of revolt that drove a great religious leader like Martin Luther into schism and heresy was not purely religious in origin, but was the outcome of a spiritual conflict in which religious motives were hopelessly confused, so that if Luther had not been such a "psychic" person, to use the word in St. Paul's sense as well as the modern one, he would have been able to judge the deep things of God as a spiritual man: he would still have been a reformer without becoming an heresiarch.

When we turn to the English Reformation, the influence of the non-religious factors in the schism is so obvious that there is no need to insist on it. It was to a great extent a movement of the State *against* the Church, and the driving force behind it was the awakening of national consciousness and the self-assertion of national culture. Hence the religious issue became so identified with the national cause that Catholicism became the representative of all the forces that were hostile to nationality, and every Catholic was regarded as a bad Englishman and a disloyal subject. To the average Englishman the typical Catholic was not Thomas More but Guy Fawkes, and the celebration of the Gunpowder Treason became a kind of primitive ritual expression of the popular detestation of the hereditary enemy of the tribe.

This identification of religion and nationality endured for more than two hundred years, and even today it remains as a subconscious prejudice at the back of men's minds. But it has inevitably tended to diminish with the growth of modern secular civilization. There is no longer any need for nationalism or class feeling or economic motives to disguise themselves in the dress of religion, for they have become the conscious and dominant forces in social life. The ideologies which today form the opposite poles of social tension are not religious, but political, national and economic ones, which have cut across and largely obliterated the older socio-religious divisions which separated Catholic and Protestant Europe.

Hence it seems to me that the present age is more favourable to the cause of unity than any time since the Middle Ages. For, if Christianity becomes a minority religion, if it is threatened by hostility and persecution, then the common cause of Christianity becomes a reality and not merely a phrase, and there is a centre round which the scattered forces of Christendom can rally and reorganize. We must remember that behind the natural process of social conflict and tension which runs through history there is a deeper law of spiritual duality and polarization which is expressed in the teaching of the Gospel on the opposition of the World and the Kingdom of God and in St. Augustine's doctrine of the two cities Babylon and Jerusalem whose conflict runs through all history and gives it its ultimate significance. When

Christians allow the conflicts and divisions of the natural man to transgress their bounds and permeate the religious sphere the cause of God becomes obscured by doubts and divisions and schism and heresies arise. But when the Church is faithful to its mission, it becomes the visible embodiment of this positive divine principle standing over against the eternal negative of evil.

I believe that the age of schism is passing and that the time has come when the divine principle of the Church's life will assert its attractive power, drawing all the living elements of Christian life and thought into organic unity. For since Christ is the Head of the Church and the Holy Spirit is the life of the Church, wherever there is faith in Christ and the Spirit of Christ there is the spirit of unity and the means of reunion. Therefore it is not necessary to talk much about the ways and means, for the ways of the Spirit are essentially mysterious and transcend human understanding. It may even be that the very strength of the forces that are gathering against the Church and against religion will make for unity by forcing Christians together, as it were, in spite of themselves; or it may be that the Church will react positively to the situation by a fresh outpouring of the apostolic spirit, as Blessed Grignon de Montfort prophesied two centuries ago.

The Building of a Christian Order

WE HAVE seen that the divisions of Christendom had their main source in social conflicts. Is it not possible to reverse the process and to find in common social action a way of return to a Christian social unity?

We are all being brought together today by the pressure of a common necessity. Our existence as free nations, our institutions and our way of life have never before been threatened as they are today. We are faced with great evils—so great that they may often seem unbearable—and yet in spite of all these evils we are being given an opportunity which is literally priceless, because it has been bought by sufferings and sacrifice that cannot be reckoned by any human scale of values. For though war destroys so much that is good, it also removes many of the obstacles and barriers which it is impossible to surmount in times of peace. It strips us of non-essentials and brings us back to the basic realities on which our common life is founded. Above all it gives us the opportunity of recovering our spiritual unity, of which we are hardly conscious in times of peace, but which is nevertheless the bedrock of our national existence.

In the past we have been a Christian people. For more than a thousand years the Christian faith has been interwoven with our history and has entered into the life and thought of ordinary men and women. We have never consciously and deliberately denied this Christian heritage. The seed is still there, though it may be mixed with weeds and choked by thorns or parched on the stony ground. And now that the harrow of war has passed over the land, it may still bear fruit, if the land is not out of heart.

In these grim times it may seem unreal to speak of the prospects of a new Christian order. But if Christianity is not suited to hard times, Christians have no right to speak at all. To build a Christian order we do not need vast economic resources or exceptionally prosperous times. Such work is better done in the spirit of Nehemias and his companions who rebuilt the ruined walls of Jerusalem without resources and in constant danger, working with one hand and holding the sword in the other. We do not need an ambitious programme of an ideal order. We must build on the foundations that still remain of human nature and national tradition. For, as the present Pope has explained in his encyclical on the war, national tradition is a kind of sacred inheritance which must not be undervalued, since, far from being opposed to the Christian ideal of the brotherhood of men, it is the natural organ by which that ideal must be realized. Now the tradition of the English-speaking peoples has always been a tradition of freedom. As Burke wrote, "all the old countries of Christian Europe were agreed on the common principle that the state is made for the people, and not the people conformed to the state, but England differed from the rest in that it made personal liberty a direct object of government and refused to sacrifice the individual to the community, or the part to the whole." Today these principles are challenged in a more fundamental way than ever before, and we are standing against an order in which all human rights and the human person itself are immolated on the altar of power to the glory of the New Leviathan.

If we are to build a Christian order for Britain it must be based on freedom, otherwise it would not be British, but it must be a Christian freedom, not a freedom of economic materialism and individual selfishness. This means that it must be a social order directed to spiritual ends, in which every man has a chance to use his freedom for the service of God according to his own powers and gifts. The liberties which we demand and which humanity demands are not the right of the strong to oppress the weak or the right of the ambitious to enrich themselves at other men's expense: but the elementary rights which are to the human spirit what air and light are to the body:—freedom to worship God, freedom of speech, freedom from want and freedom from fear. Without these man cannot be fully man, and the order that denies them is an *inhuman* Order.

The important thing to realize is that we are not fighting for any partial end or any party ideology, but in order to preserve the values of our entire social and spiritual tradition against forces that threaten to destroy it. From this point of view the use of the term

"Democracy" as the definition of our cause is not completely satisfactory. For Democracy has a restricted political significance which by no means covers the whole field of values that has to be defended, and the confusion of Democracy as a general term for our tradition of social freedom, and its more limited but more accurate political meaning, is apt to produce misunderstanding and disagreement.

For the cause that we are defending is far more fundamental than any form of government or any political creed. It is bound up with the whole tradition of Western and Christian culture—the tradition of social freedom and citizenship on the one hand, and that of spiritual freedom and the infinite value of the individual human person, on the other. No doubt Democracy as an ideal does stand for those things and is the outcome of this tradition. But in practice modern democratic culture often represents only a debased and secularized version of this ideal and in many respects, as de Tocqueville saw more than a century ago, it prepares the way for the coming of the new mass order which achieves political form in the totalitarian State. What we are defending, in short, is not democracy but humanity. The basis of our unity—the common ground on which we are all agreed—is not a matter of political opinions, it is our resistance to a system which we feel to be inhuman and opposed to everything that Christian men hold dear. We can no longer, alas! say "civilized men," for we are faced with the grim fact to which the Liberal optimism of the last century shut its eyes —the fact that a society can become inhuman, while preserving all the technical and material advantages of an advanced scientific civilization.

And in order to meet this inhuman thing we have got to adapt our life to total war and to the inhuman conditions that this involves. But how can this be done without sacrificing the very things for which the sacrifice is made? In other words, is it possible to save our lives without losing our souls? At first sight it seems easy to answer these questions in the affirmative, for this country has already gone through the experience of modern warfare and endured for four years the long drawn-out agony of Flanders and the Somme without undergoing any revolutionary transformation or losing its traditional values of humanity and fair play and personal freedom. But today the question is posed in a much more fundamental form. The loss of the peace, the failure of political democracy in post-war Europe, the rise of the totalitarian States and their successful development of the new techniques of power—all point to the insufficiency of a purely defensive policy and the necessity of a fundamental reorientation of our society and culture to meet the challenge of the new conditions of an age of scientifically organized mass power. The survival of free society is only possible if it can become as fully organized and as scientifically planned as the despotic mass order of the totalitarian States. And thus in the midst of the turmoil of war and the immediate pressure of an intensive concentration of national effort we are forced at the same time to face the fundamental long-range issue of how it is possible to plan a modern mass society without destroying social freedom and the values which Christian and Western culture has hitherto accepted as the foundation of human life.

In the first place we must recognize that it is not enough to secure religious freedom in the technical sense of the right to hold religious beliefs and to practise some kind of religious worship, for it is easy for a planned society to incorporate the least vital elements of organized Christianity at its lowest level of spiritual vitality while at the same time destroying the roots of personality without which both religion and social freedom wither and die. The totalitarian solution is to safeguard physical vitality and to sacrifice spiritual freedom. The democratic compromise is to preserve individual freedom on the superficial level of political and economic life, while disregarding both the physical and the spiritual roots.

The most important thing, therefore, is to ensure the minimum conditions that are essential for the preservation of spiritual liberty, one might even say, for the survival of the human soul: for without this neither Christian values nor the traditional values of "Western" or democratic society can be preserved.

The great danger here is that the development of the new techniques of social control (or rather perhaps the new awareness of them), has outstripped the moral and religious developments of modern culture. The negative and regressive effect of this tendency on culture has been clearly stated by Professor Karl Mannheim in *Man and Society*, but he writes from the standpoint of the planner or ruler, whereas the religious problem is best seen from the opposite stand-point—that of the subject.

If freedom is to be preserved, it is necessary also to give the individual some freedom of association and some choice of vocation. This is equally true of spiritual freedom. There must be freedom of communication or communion and freedom of vocation—especially of contemplative vocation. How are these freedoms related to one another?

In the past personal freedom has always been grounded on private property. The citizen was a man of property and consequently the franchise was restricted to those who were either freeholders or men who possessed some kind of a material status in society and some social stability. The right of property brought with it the right of freedom in the choice of an occupation. But although this right was personal it was not completely individualistic. It was bound up with the existence of a small primary group—the family—which had its possessions in common under the rule of the father—a minute communist monarchy. Thus the base of the social edifice was constituted by the family as the primary social and economic unity. Beneath and upholding politics—the Law of the city—there was economics—the Law of the household.

It was in such a social environment that the spiritual freedom of the past existed. In contrast to social and political freedom it was, however, always regarded as independent of economic relations. In fact spiritual freedom was often conceived as freedom from the bonds of property so that the vow of poverty was the normal fulfillment of the spiritual vocation. Yet political and spiritual freedom were never regarded as mutually exclusive. Indeed the latter in a sense presupposes the right of property, apart from which it loses its moral value and significance.

The fundamental and revolutionary change in modern society has been the destruction of the old personal and individual conception of property by the coming of the new order of industrial capitalism and socialism which has mechanized and depersonalized the economic basis of social life. The economic unit has grown larger and larger and has become increasingly assimilated to the organized public services which have always existed (e.g. army, civil service, government work shops and engineering departments), but which in the past were exceptional and sharply contrasted with the sphere of private economic activity.

Property is increasingly separated from work and becomes above all the right to receive income from large-scale enterprises that are administered by salaried professionals.

In such a society it is clear that there is far less room for personal choice than under the earlier system. In the days of mercenary armies, a man was free to take service in the Austrian or the Hanoverian or the Swedish forces and he was free to choose also the form of service and the regiment he preferred. Under universal conscription, on the other hand, he became a number in a register, a piece of raw material which is measured and classified before it is put into the machine.

And the same is true of men's work, in the socialist and totalitarian state. The individual is drafted into his place in the economic machine when he leaves school. The more perfectly the system is planned, the more completely will the individual be conditioned and adapted to perform his economic function. But while there is no room for individual freedom which would interfere with the working of the machine, it is equally undesirable that there should be a sense of restraint which would generate resistance or inefficiency. It will therefore be the purpose of society to condition the individual for total service to the community, and in fact the totalitarian systems have gone a long way to achieving this aim.

Nevertheless this solution is so opposed to the whole tradition of Western and Christian culture that it is almost inconceivable that it can be accepted by our civilization. In fact we may well ask whether the present crisis from which the world is suffering is not due to instinctive reaction of Western society against a system which is destructive of its innermost being and the roots of its spiritual vitality. And the reason this is not more obvious is because the disease has gone so far. Already in the nineteenth century the capitalist order admitted the triumph of economic man and the subordination of the spiritual elements in Western culture to material ends, so that it was no longer morally in a position to withstand the attack of the totalitarian revolution. Marx was perfectly right when he claimed that the capitalist bourgeoisie was cutting the ground from under its feet and producing its own grave diggers. Where he went wrong was in

his prophecy of the inevitable victory of the proletariat. The same grave was destined to receive them
both, and the victorious power was not the brotherhood of free workers, but the impersonal tyranny of
the machine order, which is an order of destruction
no less than of production—an order of production
for destruction which finds its supreme expression in
mechanized warfare and in total world war.

The monstrous nature of this development renders
it intolerable to every sane mind. Everybody agrees in
principle that the machine order must be humanized,
if civilization is to survive. It is not enough to social-
ize it—to equalize its pressure on the classes and individual members of the community, for that simply
means equality in slavery. It is necessary to recognize
the dangers of dehumanization that are inherent in a
mechanized order and to take deliberate measures
to protect human nature from the impersonal forces
that tend to overwhelm it. In other words civilization
must be replanned from the opposite end to that
from which the capitalist and communist and totalitarian organization has proceeded. The elements in
society that have hitherto been left to take care of
themselves must become the elements most carefully
protected and most highly valued.

What are these elements? First, freedom of association, the principle which has always distinguished
the free citizen community of classical antiquity and
modern Europe from the servile state in which the
individual is regarded merely as a subject.

Secondly, freedom of vocation which is the condition of personal responsibility. This freedom is not

the same as the competitive freedom of economic man, which usurped its place in the eighteenth and nineteenth centuries—the freedom of trade and industry and the right of the individual to direct his activities to his private profit. On the contrary, vocation and profit are opposite motives, since the former involves a certain disinterestedness which subordinates the profit motive to a non-economic end. In the case of a religious vocation, this is so obvious that it is unnecessary to labour the point. And it is also clear in the case of the professions, which fulfill a recognized social function and possess a tradition of disinterested service.

The most famous example of this is the medical profession which from the beginning has been inspired by the high ideal of disinterested service that finds classical expression in the formula of the Hippocratic oath. But a similar sense of vocation and professional honour has existed in the past to a greater or less degree among scientists and soldiers, scholars and lawyers, craftsmen and shepherds. It was the great evil of capitalist culture to weaken or destroy this spirit and to substitute the profit motive and the power of money as the supreme standards of social life. And now that the profit motive is being ousted by the ideal of technical efficiency and the power of money is being dethroned by the power of the State, the need for a restoration of the ethics of vocation has become the central problem of society. If Mammon is to be dethroned, in order that Moloch be set in his place, the new order will be more inhuman and more anti-Christian than the old. And this is what, in fact, we see in the totalitarian State.

The revolutionaries have not ignored the importance of the two social elements of which I write. Communism has founded itself upon the ideal of comradeship which is the principle of association. Fascism has founded itself on the ideal of leadership which is that of vocation. But both alike have denied freedom, and therefore the cult of leadership becomes a demonic worship of power and the cult of comradeship becomes an excuse for the subjection of the individual to the ruthless dictatorship of a party.

Our society still preserves a strong tradition of social and political freedom and it is this, rather than equality or the divine right of majorities, which is the essence of what we call democracy. But we no less than the totalitarian states, are undergoing the process of social and economic change from the unregulated freedom of nineteenth-century capitalism to the mechanized order of a planned society. Hitherto we have escaped the bitterness of class conflict and the revolutionary violence that have accompanied the process elsewhere. It has been carried out by the gradual and constitutional extension of bureaucratic control in every field of social activity, and so long as the system is not shattered by the external catastrophe of military defeat there seems no reason why the process should not continue until our society is as completely planned as any totalitarian State.

Can freedom survive such a process? There is obviously a danger that bureaucratic planning may destroy freedom no less completely than totalitarian dictatorship. Nevertheless it is not necessary and inevitable, since the system is not in itself irreconcilable with the principle of freedom of vocation. Indeed, the civil servant is better fitted than the business man or the politician to represent the principle of disinterested service and professional honor in modern society as against the capitalist motive of profit and the dictatorial will to power. In the past, it is true, it has been the negative elements in bureaucracy that have been most evident, with the result that it has become associated in the popular mind with red tape and formalism, with the avoidance of personal responsibility and the love of routine. But this was largely due to the cramped and narrowing conditions of the age of individualism when the public service was restricted by the Whig tradition of aristocratic privilege on the one hand, and by the Liberal prejudice against State interference on the other.

There has been such an immense expansion in the functions and power of bureaucracy that it is as far removed from what it was a century ago, as the official hierarchy of the age of Diocletian was from the civil service of the early empire. Nevertheless our society has not yet assimilated the change, and public opinion is still influenced by habits of thought which belonged to traditions that have long ceased to exist. The public servant has not yet fully realized the extent of his responsibility. It is not enough to be a competent and hardworking specialist. Nothing could be higher in that respect than the standard of the German bureaucracy. Yet for that very reason it was the obedient servant of whatever power happened by whatever means to gain control of the State.

The immense growth in the power of the administration which is characteristic of every modern State must be accompanied by a corresponding growth in the sense of personal responsibility on the part of the administrators, otherwise it will become an impersonal rule of slaves over slaves: the tyranny of the slaves of the bureau over the slaves of the machine. In other words the public servant must himself be a freeman and a citizen, if he is to administer a free society. As we have seen, it is the tendency of the new order to treat both economic organization and politics as forms of public service, so that the civil service becomes the standard and pattern of the whole social structure. Consequently if the principle of freedom of vocation is preserved at this point, it will secure spiritual freedom at the key point, whereas if it is lost here, the whole of society will become mechanized and lifeless.

It is true that this is not the only principle at stake, since freedom of vocation without freedom of association is impossible or meaningless. But we still possess a large measure of freedom of this latter kind, even though it is increasingly restricted by the mechanization of economic life. We have not yet lost the sense of citizenship and there are still wide tracts of social life in which the principle of free association can find expression; e.g. in the spontaneous creation of new groups and organizations to meet new social needs, as we have seen during the last year in our bombed cities.

This, however, only gives us the raw material of a free society. Left to itself the principle of association may expend itself in an anarchic proliferation of rival and overlapping groups, or it may degenerate into an exploitation of group selfishness in which comradeship becomes an excuse for graft and corruption. It is only when it is informed by the spirit of vocation and individual responsibility that freedom of association becomes capable of serving the higher order of culture and creating the conditions under which man's freedom is spiritually fruitful, so that instead of a dead bureaucracy controlling a formless mass activity we have the organic form of a living community. In the capitalist age the profit motive was so overemphasized that society tended to become a soulless and heartless organization which was no more capable of evoking men's love and loyalty than a joint stock company. In the totalitarian State the power motive is so overemphasized that it swallows up everything else and destroys not only freedom but the elementary decencies of life. Both alike make for exploitation—the exploitation of the weak by the strong and the many by the few—whether the strong are represented by the holders of economic power, as in capitalist society, or by the holders of political power—the party bosses and the State police in the totalitarian system.

It is only by strengthening the element of vocation both in the State and in society generally that these evils can be avoided. It was the strength of the English political system in the past, that in spite of its spirit of class privilege it did regard politics as a form of public service and not as an opportunity to share out the spoils of power—that this attitude set the tone to the public services and the professions so that a high standard of personal integrity and responsibility was taken for granted. It is remarkable that when in the first half of the nineteenth century a great French writer set out to portray the principle of duty and disinterested service against the motive of power and ambition and military glory he chose an English admiral who was his country's enemy as the embodiment of his ideal.*

It is clear that if England is to adapt herself to the discipline of a planned society, it is this element, above all others, in the national tradition which provides the necessary moral dynamic. Our national temperament is naturally rebellious to the Prussian spirit of drilled obedience and methodical organization from above, and still more to the mass mysticism which makes it easy for the Slav to abandon himself in ecstatic self-surrender to an impersonal collective power. But, on the other hand, it is easier for the English to accept the idea of social duty and disinterested service with a sense of personal responsibility. If this spirit can be applied to the new conditions of mass society, it is conceivable that a planned society might be created without the destruction of freedom either by impersonal bureaucracy or by inhuman tyranny. But the task to be achieved is so great that it cannot be accomplished by political and social means alone. It involves the action of deeper spiritual forces

* I.e. the idealized portrait of Admiral Collingwood in Alfred de Vigny's *Servitude et Grandeur Militaires*.

which belong to the religious sphere. If our civilization is so completely secularized that the intervention of these forces is impossible then, I believe, there is no hope of preserving freedom and the new order will be increasingly impersonal and inhuman. But if Christianity is still a living power in the world, it must still form the ultimate basis of the restoration of human freedom and personal responsibility.

The capitalist order which is based on the power of money and the motive of profit was profoundly alien from Christian values and was the main cause of the secularization of our culture. The totalitarian order which is based on the cult of power marks a reversion to pre-Christian standards and finds its appropriate religious experience in some form of neo-paganism. But an order founded on the principle of vocation has a natural affinity with Christian ideals. In fact it is in the Christian idea of spiritual vocation that the conception of social vocation finds its archetype and pattern. We see this affinity from the beginning in the relations between the Christian apostles and the representatives of the Roman order, so that Peter and Paul, the chosen of the Lord, seem to have felt for Cornelius the Centurion and Festus the Governor a kind of instinctive understanding which they did not feel either for the Jewish priests or the Greek philosophers. They saw them as men who were doing disinterested service in their own calling and therefore ministers of God even as they themselves, though on a lower plane of action.

It is in the religious sphere that the principle of freedom and vocation finds its fullest and most per-

fect development, as we see in the wonderful chapters
of St. Paul's first epistle to the Corinthians in which
he compares the difference of spiritual gifts and operations in the Church with the functions of the natural
organism (1 Cor. XII, 4-27 inc.).

Now there are diversities of graces, but the same
Spirit. And there are diversities of ministries, but the
same Lord. And there are diversities of operations, but
the same God, who worketh all in all. And the manifestation of the Spirit is given to every man's profit. To
one indeed, by the Spirit, is given the word of wisdom: and to another, the word of knowledge, according to the same Spirit: to another, faith in the same
spirit: to another, the grace of healing in one Spirit:
to another, the working of miracles: to another, prophecy: to another, the discerning of spirits: to another, di-
vers kinds of tongues: to another, interpretation of
speeches. But all these things, one and the same Spirit
worketh, dividing to every one according as he will. For
as the body is one and hath many members; and all the
members of the body, whereas they are many, yet are
one body: so also is Christ. For in one Spirit were we all
baptized into one body, whether Jews or Gentiles,
whether bond or free: and in one Spirit we have all been
made to drink. For the body also is not one member, but
many. If the foot should say: Because I am not the hand,
I am not of the body: Is it therefore not of the body?
And if the ear should say: Because I am not the eye, I
am not of the body: Is it therefore not of the body? If
the whole body were the eye, where would be the hearing? If the whole body were the hearing, where would
be the smelling? But now God hath set the members,
every one of them, in the body as it hath pleased him.

And if they all were one member, where would be the body? But now there are many members indeed, yet one body. And the eye cannot say to the hand: I need not thy help. Nor again the head to the feet: I have no need of you. Yea, much more those that seem to be the more feeble members of the body are more necessary. And such as we think to be the less honourable members of the body, about these we put more abundant honour: and those that are our uncomely parts have more abundant comeliness. But our comely parts have no need; but God hath tempered the body together, giving to that which wanted the more abundant honour. That there might be no schism in the body; but the members might be mutually careful one for another. And if one member suffer any thing, all the members suffer with it: or if one member glory, all the members rejoice with it. Now you are the body of Christ and members of one another.

And St. Paul then goes on to show that beyond all the spiritual gifts, transcending and fulfilling them, there is the one universal and indispensable way of charity, the heart of the spiritual organism without which the highest and the most powerful spiritual gifts become worthless and lifeless.

Now the same conception of the organic life of the community and the same principles of order and vocation and functional differentiation were applied to the State and the social order by Christian thinkers, and became the basis of Christian social ethics in the Middle Ages, so that St. Thomas sees society as a cosmos of vocations in which every particular social and economic function finds its place in the universal order of ends. And this conception permeated Western culture so deeply that it was not entirely destroyed either by the Reformation or the individualism of the capitalist age, but retained its vitality and was finally reasserted in the social encyclicals of Leo XIII and Pius XI.

It is true that the relevance of this conception has been to some extent obscured by the fact that it was first developed against the social background of feudalism with a partriarchal tradition of authority, so that it is always apt to be given a conservative and undemocratic bias. We have seen in our own days how the principles of organism and function have been exploited in the interests of Fascism and Nazism, though there can in reality be no reconciliation between the inhuman mechanism of the totalitarian State and the principle of freedom of vocation. For just as spiritual vocation in the religious sense presupposes the freedom of the Spirit and the bond of charity, so the principle of vocation in the temporal sphere demands personal freedom and the right of free association, without which the order of the State and the economic order, however highly organized they may be, become orders of slavery.

6

Christendom, Europe and the New World

THE principle of vocation of which I have written in the last chapter is no less important for international order than it is for the life of the state and the community. If we trace the idea of vocation back to its original source in the Christian tradition, we find that from the first it had a twofold character, and that the spiritual vocation of the individual was inseparably linked with the historical mission of a people. For the calling of Abraham, "the friend of God," was also the calling of a chosen people set apart for a world mission. And throughout the Old Testament we find the prophets insisting, not only on the divine vocation of Israel, but also on the calling of particular nations and empires to fulfil some particular task in world history.

It is true that in the New Testament the emphasis is rather on the breaking down of national barriers and the universality of the Gospel—that "God has made of one blood all nations of men that dwell on the face of the earth"—and that in Christ there is "neither Jew nor Greek, neither bond nor free, neither male nor female." It was only in the Church that this ultimate fact of the unity and brotherhood of the human race was realized and expressed. The Christians were "a chosen race, a royal priesthood, a holy nation, a people for God's own possession."* or, as the Epistle to Diognetus puts it "what the soul is in the body, that the Christians are in the world." "The soul is spread through all members of the body and Christians throughout the cities of the world. . . . The soul is confined in the body, but itself sustains the body; and Christians are confined in the world as in a ward, but themselves sustain the world. . . . God has appointed to them so great a post, and it is not right for them to decline it."**

The history of Christendom is the history of a culture based on this idea of spiritual universalism— which was more than an idea, because it was embodied in the superpolitical society of the Church. With the conversion, first of the Roman Empire and then of the barbarians, there was formed a community of peoples sharing a common spiritual tradition which was transmitted from age to age and from people to people until it embraced the whole of Europe. More than this, it created Europe. For the European continent is the result of the European culture and not vice versa. From the physical point of view Europe is not a unity but simply the north western extension of the Asiatic land mass. Nor is it a racial unity, for from prehistoric times it has been a melting pot of races and a meeting ground of cultural traditions of the most diverse origin. The formal principle of European unity is not physical but

* *1 Peter* 3.9.
** *Epistle to Diognetus* 6.

spiritual. Europe was Christendom: it was the society of Christian peoples which for a thousand years, more or less, had been molded by the same religious and intellectual influence until it possessed a consciousness of spiritual community which transcended political and racial limits. As long as this spiritual community was recognized as a concrete social reality there was no room for the modern ideal of nationality and even the political unit held a relatively humble place. Kings and princes were regarded as officers in the Christian commonwealth, not sovereigns in the Austinian sense, and the very name of the State—state, état, Staat—as the ultimate community which forms the basis of all modern social thinking originates with the Italian publicists of the Renaissance who were in conscious revolt against the whole tradition of medieval Christendom. In fact it was in the sinister connotation of *raison d'état— raggione di stata*—that the new term acquired general currency in Western Europe.

Nevertheless it is not satisfactory to explain the rise of the national state merely as a revolt against the unity of Christendom and the traditions of Christian culture, for each and all of them retained a certain allegiance to these traditions and a common European consciousness. Each of the great European states was, in fact, a microcosm of the universal Christian society from which they had emerged. They represent a crystallization of the different social and cultural elements round a power centre, which was a pole of cultural as well as political forces. Thus there arose two opposed yet complementary attitudes towards the state and the nation. On the one hand, it was recognized that the community was part of a wider whole, a part of Europe, a member of the society of nations; on the other hand, the fact that each of the great powers regarded itself as the heir and guardian of the universal ideal of Christendom caused them to realize their national vocation as a chosen people with a special mission to the world. Italy, France, Spain, England, Germany, Russia, Poland, Ireland—all of them at one time or another, and sometimes simultaneously, have cherished this idea of a particular vocation or mission which sometimes, as in nineteenth century Poland, has assumed a definitely Messianic form, but more often expresses itself aggressively in the form of imperialism or national aggrandizement.

It was of decisive importance for this development that the breaking down of the society of medieval Christendom and the rise of the new state coincided with the age of discovery and the opening of new worlds to European colonization and exploitation. While the old cradle lands of Western culture in the Eastern Mediterranean were being violently torn away from the rest of Europe by the Ottoman conquest, new and unlimited fields of expansion were being opened to the young peoples of the West in America and Africa and South Eastern Asia. The example of Spain and Portugal was rapidly followed by the Netherlands and England and France so that the whole orientation of Europe was shifted from its old Mediterranean axis to the new Atlantic world. Moreover, Muscovite Russia which had been living withdrawn for centuries in dependence on the Mongol empire finally checked the immemorial westward drift of the warrior peoples of the steppes and began to expand into Northern Asia, while at the same time she recovered contact with Western Europe and came increasingly under the influence of Western culture. Thus by the nineteenth century Europe had come to be the mistress of the world. European civilization was regarded as "civilization" in an absolute sense. European science and techniques, European political institutions and ideas, even European dress and manners had become universalized and transformed the lives of millions of people who had been living hitherto in obedience to the sacred traditions of ancient civilizations or under the prehistoric conditions of primitive barbarism. Everywhere from the American prairie to the African jungle virgin lands were being appropriated by European adventurers and the natural resources of the world were being exploited by European prospectors and engineers to provide dividends for European shareholders and food for European workers.

But this world expansion of European culture was accompanied by a centrifugal movement which disintegrated European unity and produced, on the one hand, a generalized cosmopolitan culture which had its roots in Europe, but no close organic relation to it, and on the other, a new cult of nationality which left no room for any wider community. This new cult found its fullest and most intense expression in Germany during the national awakening that followed the Napoleonic Conquest, but it was not exclusively German in origin and its subsequent development embraced the whole of Europe and was carried from one end of the world to the other as an inseparable part of Western ideology. Nevertheless in its earlier Romantic form nationalism did not imply any hostility to the idea of Europe. It is significant that the German writer who first coined the word Nationality was Novalis, the author of *Die Christenheit oder Europa*, which looks back to the unity of medieval Christendom as a pattern for the reorganization of Europe and humanity. It was only when nationalism became detached from this romantic idealism and reinterpreted in terms of popular Darwinian biology that it acquired a definitely anti-European character. Nevertheless in Germany above all nationalism continued to retain a certain quasi-religious appeal, and it is this incongruous fusion of racialist materialism and nationalist mysticism which has produced the portentous social phenomenon of National Socialism, as we see it today.

Here the state is no longer regarded as the member of a society of nations but as existing solely to further the ends of the racial community which is the ultimate social reality. Between these ultimate units there is no community, for nature demands that each should keep rigidly within the limits of its own life forms. Therefore the mingling of races and cultures is the supreme social crime. The purer the race, the higher the culture, and the final law of human progress is to be found in the victorious expansion of the higher types and the progressive elimination of the lower races.

It is obvious that these theories are well fitted to provide an ideological basis for the aggressive policy of a military imperialism, and we see in the case of Germany and Japan at the present moment what tremendous driving power can be generated by the self-exaltation of a highly organized national community. Nevertheless they offer no hope for world order, since they stand in direct contradiction to the whole traditions and ethos of Western civilization, which even Hitler himself regards as the source of man's highest achievement.* For, as we have seen, it was the spiritual community that created European unity and it was as a community of culture that Western civilization acquired its world-wide influence. It is true that Europe was also a society of nations and that therefore the racial element, the bond of common blood, like the bond of common speech and common fatherland, played an important part in its development. But both civilization and nation are like chemical compounds which owe their very existence to their synthesis and any attempt to resolve them into their compound elements involves their destruction. Hence the new racialism is but another symptom of the disintegration of our culture. The dissolution of the European unity has caused men to concentrate first on the parts which constitute it—the nations—and then on the elements from which the nations were compounded.

---

* Cf. his interesting remarks on Japan and Western Culture in *Mein Kampf*, pt. I, ch. xi.

Thus the racialist ideology, like the Communist ideology, is a result of the break-down of European unity and of the attempt to find a substitute for it in some primary social element which is permanent and indestructible. But if, as we believe, Europe was essentially a spiritual unity, based on religion and expressed in culture, it cannot be replaced by a biological or economic unit, for these belong to a different plane of social reality. They are social elements, not social organisms in the full sense.

It is true that it is impossible to restore the old European order, even in its most recent and most loosely organized form, for modern economic development and modern mechanized warfare have profoundly affected the conditions of political life and the conception of state sovereignty, so that it is no longer possible for the lesser states of Europe to maintain their independence by the traditional system of military alliances and the balance of power. But this does not mean that they should be sacrificed to the will to power of totalitarian mass states or absorbed in a racial unity which may be an artificial creation of a nationalist propaganda. Small states like Switzerland and Belgium which do not even speak a common language may nevertheless possess a strong national character and historic traditions which cannot be denied in the interests of any racial theory or party ideology. For it is by the life of historic societies of this kind whether great or small that European civilization exists. Even today the national traditions and the social unity of the European peoples seem as strong as ever; the failure has been on the political plane, it is the failure of the individual state and the European state system as a whole to adapt themselves to the new conditions.

Yet even this failure is an indirect testimony to the powers of Western civilization since it is the result of the world expansion of Western culture and its triumph over the physical limitations which conditioned civilization in the past. Down to the beginning of the twentieth century international politics were still a closed field reserved to the European powers and the rest of the world provided a passive background for their manoeuvres. We have still hardly adjusted our minds to the enlarged scale of world politics or envisaged the possibility of a world order in which the unit is not the state but the civilization.

But with the coming of the present war we have seen the old state-system falling to pieces under the massive assaults of a single totalitarian power, while the struggle of giant superstates continues over the prostrate body of Europe. At the present moment there remain only six centers of world power: Germany, Italy, the USSR, Japan, the United States and the British Commonwealth—three unitary military powers against three great federations,* while the potential seventh world power—China—is almost submerged by the mounting tide of Japanese conquest. With the exception of Italy, which owes its importance almost entirely to its dependence on another

---

* I use the word in the sense of "a polity in which a number of states form a unity but remain independent in internal affairs." (Cf. Concise Oxford Dictionary s.v. federation.)

power, none of these powers is a nation state in the traditional sense. They are either military empires or federations embracing millions of square miles of territory and hundreds of millions of inhabitants. The USA extends from the Atlantic to the Pacific, the USSR from the Pacific to the Baltic, while the British Commonwealth is a world society which extends into all the five continents. It is obvious that the development of these vast superstates entirely upsets the delicate balance of power on which the old European state system was based. The only possible international order today is a world order which includes all the great centers of world power and organizes international security on a universal basis.

This was recognized in principle by the founders of the League of Nations, but as we have seen in chapter five, they failed to take account of the new forces and created an organization which was neither European nor universal, since it included neither the USA nor the USSR and since its real basis was a system of alliances, similar to those which had guaranteed the European balance of power in the eighteenth and nineteenth centuries. It is not surprising that a system which ignored the realities of world power should have been defied and wrecked by the new régimes in Europe and Asia which based themselves on the naked reality of power and ignored every other factor. But though racialism, militarism, autarky and unlimited aggression are powerful as revolutionary and destructive forces, they cannot be used as foundations of a new order. The work of the League of Nations has to be done over again with greater realism and wider responsibility. It cannot be done by Europe alone, but it cannot be done without Europe, since Europe still represents the greatest concentration of population and power and cultural activity in the world. Moreover it is from Europe and from America, which is Europe's New World, that the very idea of an international world order has come, and it is through Western influence and in communion with Western culture that the peoples of Asia and Africa have become conscious of their world citizenship and their international status.

But is it possible to conceive of any solution which will reconcile the rights of nations with the existence of Europe, on the one hand, and the need of world order, on the other? In the first place, it is necessary to bear in mind that the problem is not that of a single relationship between the nation and the League of Nations or the state and the world society. It is a threefold relationship, involving a cultural unity which is intermediate between the nation and the world. Hitherto the cultural unit has been the ultimate one, and the different cultures and civilizations, such as China and Europe for example, were closed worlds, with the same attitude to one another as that of the Greeks and the Barbarians in antiquity, or Christians and Moslem in the Middle Ages. But the new world that we see today is a civilization of civilizations, a world society made up of different culture provinces, each of which in turn is made up of a number of different peoples or nations. Almost all existing social and political ideologies ignore the existence of this intermediate group and see the state as the supreme social reality against the background of a formless and inorganic international society which is simply the sum of all the states in the world. But a true world order must take account not merely of the realities of power but of the realities of culture, which affect not only political and social institutions but men's view of life and the archetypes of their social experience.

There are two lines on which this problem might be dealt with. On the one hand, each civilization or culture area might be organized as an autocratic world under the empire of a totalitarian superstructure. This is the solution of Germany and Japan, and it is equally unsatisfactory from the point of view of the rights of nations as from that of the peace of the world. The alternative solution is to create not a league of nations but a confederation, a league of federations, based on community of culture and each organized as a society of nations or states with autonomous rights.

We already possess examples of this type of political organism in the three world powers which are allied in the present struggle, different as they are in constitution and historical traditions. The USA is a federation which has become a national unity, while the British Commonwealth and the USSR are empires which have developed into federations. All of them profess similar democratic ideals and reject the principle of racial inequality, though the application of these ideals is limited in the USSR by the totalitarian character of the Communist ideology and methods of revolutionary dictatorship, and in the

British Empire by the difference of status between the self-governing dominions and the colonial territories and protectorates, as well as by the inclusion of the vast subcontinent of India, which forms one of the great world culture-areas and one of the potential members of the world confederation. For India is not a nation, it is a society of nations like Europe, with a common tradition of civilization which transcends politics and which has survived countless invasions and centuries of foreign domination.

But what of Europe itself? Is it possible to conceive of a Western European federation which would take its place with the three existing federal unities, as a member of the world society? At the present moment the ideal of a United States of Europe may seem Utopian and unreal, yet it seems the only solution capable of reconciling the national freedom and cultural autonomy of the Western European peoples with the tradition of European unity and the needs of world order.

The objections to the idea of a European federation are largely the result of taking too narrow a view of the nature of federation, and conceiving it in terms of the USA where the federal solution was rendered possible by the fact that national sentiment was concentrated on the Union itself rather than on the States which possessed a provincial rather than a national character. But in Europe the intensive development of national political traditions and national culture has made every people so conscious of its own individuality that any limitation of its political sovereignty is felt as a threat to its spiritual being.

It seems absurd to conclude from this that the only possible form of European unity is a totalitarian imperialism which would destroy all national freedom. It is surely more reasonable to think that the organization of Europe should be as free and as diversified as possible. The British Commonwealth of Nations has shown how far it is possible to go in the direction of autonomy and diversity of the constituent parts while preserving a real, though indefinite social and political unity. It is like our hypothetical world order a federation of federations, and moreover one which exists with a minimum of central organization and control. In the same way it is possible to conceive of a European union which would be primarily a society of free peoples, in which small and great states, kingdoms and republics with their own institutions and constitutions existed side by side with one another, as do the members of the British Commonwealth of Nations.

Such a federation would be entirely consistent with the traditional conception of European unity, which Burke defined as a commonwealth of Christian nations, based on a common way of life, a community of culture, and possessing a common public law.

The political value of this conception was vitiated by the acceptance of war as a normal part of international law, a vice which was limited but not cured by the attempt of Grotius to define the conditions of a just war. It is true that, partly under the influence of Burke's ideas, a serious attempt was made in 1815 to unite the states of Europe on the basis of

Christian principles, as members of the Christian family of nations. But since the scheme was launched by the three great autocratic states of Eastern Europe and ignored the principles of nationality and the rights of peoples its sublime ideals were dismissed as a mask for tyranny and were destroyed by the nationalist movements of the mid-nineteenth-century which completely failed to take account of the need for an organized European order.

Today this need is realized on every side and the real issue is not between a German or Anglo-American or Russian hegemony of Europe, but whether Europe is to be organized as a totalitarian military empire or as a free democratic federation. It is only by the second alternative that it is possible to integrate the principle of national self-determination in a wider unity which would possess sufficient community of culture and historic tradition to arouse a real sense of loyalty, such as an international organization like the League of Nations is unable to create. A European union of this kind would be in a position to co-operate with the other world federations— the British Commonwealth, the USA and the USSR as well as with Latin America and India and China as a constituent member of a federal world order.

In this way it would be possible to preserve the national character and cultural mission of the lesser states which tend to disappear in the cosmopolitan atmosphere of a world state. Thus Switzerland or Denmark each has its place and significance in the European order, like Colombia or Ecuador in Latin America, or New Zealand or Newfoundland in the

British Commonwealth, and their individual values would be lost or seriously impaired in a uniform world system, in which the small state is incorporated as an isolated unit, side by side with giant super-states that number their population by the hundred million.

No doubt the difficulties that stand in the way of the creation of this organic federal system of world order are immense, but the same is true of any system of world order from a League of Nations to a unitary world state. Yet the catastrophic history of the last thirty years with its two world wars and its succession of political and economic crises ought to supply enough proof to convince the most cautious and conservative mind that the question of world order is not a utopian speculation but a vital issue on which our own lives and the existence of our civilization depend. At the present time the forces of destruction and violence are temporarily in the ascendent, so that men are tempted to abandon the principles on which Western civilization has been based and to surrender themselves to the demonic powers that have emerged from beneath the rationalized surface of modern society. This is the great tragedy of our time: that the aggressive policy and propaganda of amoral power appeals to deeper elements in the mass consciousness than does the moral idealism of international justice and universal peace. And therefore it is only by the recovery of a dynamic spiritual force which moves the conscience of society more deeply than the material will to power that mankind can be saved from its peril.

We have seen that European civilization owed its origin neither to racial unity nor to political organization but to the spiritual forces which united Romans and barbarians in the new society of Christendom. But that society was not limited in principle to the particular society of peoples of which it was actually composed. It was in principle a universal society, based on the unity and brotherhood of mankind and corresponding on the temporal plane to the new idea of humanity which transcended all divisions of race and class, "in which there is neither Greek nor Jew, circumcised nor uncircumcised, Barbarian nor Scythian, bond nor free, but Christ is all and in all." If this faith is still alive in the world today it is no less valid as a spiritual basis of world order, as it was in the past for the making of Europe; in fact, it is only in a world order that the Christian social idea finds its full expression, since from the beginning the ideal of spiritual universalism and the world vocation of Christianity have formed the background of Christian social ethics. Thus Christians have a twofold responsibility and mission in the present crisis. In the first place they are the heirs of the old European tradition and the guardians of the spiritual principle from which Europe derived its being. There is nothing in the European past that has not been formed or conditioned by Christian influences, and even the heresiarchs and the revolutionaries are not to be excepted since they have often been inspired by an exaggerated and one-sided devotion to some particular element in the common tradition. And in the second place Christians have a new responsibility and mission to the new world society that Europe has created in spite of itself by its scientific achievements and its colonial and economic expansion. This world society is still formless, a chaos in which the forces of destruction alone seem active. It does not possess in itself any principle of order or spiritual power which is capable of giving it organic form and unity. Any attempt to organize the world by military or economic power divorced from spiritual vision is doomed to failure, because it ignores the deepest and most vital factors in the problem, and if these psychological and spiritual factors are neglected they are apt to reassert themselves in a destructive and passionate revolt such as that which destroyed the Weimar republic and the international system of the League of Nations.

It is therefore impossible to dismiss the claims of Christianity as irrelevant to the problem of international order, for the demonic powers which have entered the empty house of secular civilization are not to be exorcised by the economist or the politician: religion is the only power that can meet the forces of destruction on equal terms and save mankind from its spiritual enemies.

The world mission of Christianity is based on its conception of a spiritual society which transcends all states and cultures and is the final goal of humanity. Wherever Christianity exists there survives a seed of unity, a principle of spiritual order, which cannot be destroyed by war or the conflict of economic interests or the failure of political organization. No doubt it will be said that the Christian Church does not in fact perform this function, and that Christians are too few, too weak and too poor in intellectual and spiritual qualities to influence the course of history. But the same might have been said of the Jews in the age of the prophets or of the Christians themselves under the Roman Empire. "You see your vocation, brethren," wrote St. Paul, "that not many wise men according to the flesh, not many of the powerful, not many of the noble are called." It is of the very nature of Christianity not to depend on human means, not to trust in "the arm of the flesh," not to judge events by human or secular standards. The one thing that it demands is faith, and lack of faith is the only thing that even defeats the divine purpose.

Thus the hope of the world rests in the last resort on the existence of a spiritual nucleus of believers who are the bearers of the seed of unity. Each has its special and unique contribution to make to the life of the whole. But in the present state of world disorder where each society strives to achieve its purpose by political power without reference to the rights of others or the life of the whole, their vocation is frustrated, so that the higher and the more unique it is, the more absolute is the opposition and the more bitter the conflict. The reconciliation of the nations can only be accomplished on a deeper plane than that of political power or economic interest. It is essentially a spiritual task which demands the spiritual vision that is faith and the spiritual will that is charity. We see today what happens to the world when the spirit of hatred becomes the driving power behind the vast state machine that has been built up by modern scientific organization. In face of this evil, all political differences and all differences of class or nationality or race fade into insignificance. Even the evils of the present war, enormous though they be, are but the outward and visible signs of the "mystery of lawlessness" which is at work in the world today.

The power of the Spirit is the only power that is strong enough to overcome it. In its strength Christians in the past faced and overcame the pagan civilization of the Roman Empire and the pagan savagery of their barbarian conquerors. The new paganism that we have to face today is more terrible than either of these in its cold inhumanity and its scientific exploitation of evil.

But if we have faith in the power of the Spirit we must believe that even these evils can be conquered. For the powers of the world, formidable as they appear, are blind powers which are working in the dark, and which derive their strength from negative and destructive forces. They are powerless against that Spirit who is the Lord and Giver of Life. And in the same way all their new and elaborate devices for the enslavement of the human mind are powerless against those higher powers of spiritual understanding and love which are the essential gifts of the Holy Spirit.

5